MAKERS OF HISTORY

SIR
WALTER
RALEIGH

by

PHILIP MAGNUS

COLLINS

St James's Place, London

First published in 1956
First published in the 'Makers of History' Series 1968

Sir Walter Raleigh and his son Wat,

by an unknown artist, 1602

Contents

Plates

Maps

Acknowledgments

The author and publishers wish to thank the
following for permission to use material as illus-
trations: The National Portrait Gallery for the
frontispiece and Plates 1, 2, 3, 5 and 6; the Mansell
Collection for Plate 4.

PREFACE

Raleigh and the Sixteenth Century

Q UEEN ELIZABETH, as the inveterate gossip and
antiquary John Aubrey observed, loved to sur-
round herself with ' proper men ', and Sir Walter
Raleigh's ' graceful presence was no mean recom-
mendation '. All accounts agree that he looked
magnificent in his uniform as Captain of the Yeomen
of the Guard. He was ' a tall, handsome, bold
man ', but ' damnable proud '. His figure was
beautifully proportioned, and he had, if Aubrey
can be trusted, ' an exceeding high forehead, long-
faced and sour eye-lidded, a kind of pig-eye. His
beard turned up naturally '. He had a swarthy
complexion and exquisite hands. He was extraordinarily versatile, as soldier, sailor, courtier, wit,
colonist, explorer, poet, historian, chemist, politician,
administrator, and leader of men; and he combined
in one brilliant and attractive person the main
motives of an age of expanding horizons and uni-
versal change.

Those motives may be symbolized by an open

Bible, a sailing-ship, and a Greek or Latin grammar. The Bible inspired Luther's successors towards the ultimate goal of freedom to worship God in any way they chose; the ship carried the successors of Columbus to the wealth and romance of the New World; the grammar, by familiarizing scholars with Greek and Latin authors, reopened to mankind the fearless speculations of the ancient, pagan world.

The sixteenth century, into the midst of which Raleigh was born, was being fertilized by a stream of new material wealth and intellectual experience. That gave rise to a great inventiveness, and inspired unforgettable responses to the demand for a more varied and richer mental life. The structure of society was becoming increasingly differentiated, and the gap between highest and lowest was widening. But on that undemocratic basis rested the principal achievements of that age—' the voyages, the colonial experiments, the building, the arts, the conspicuous consumption . . . the interesting extravagance upon luxuries that have lasted, jewels, stuffs, fabrics, music; the demand for books, literature, the drama . . .' [1] There were glittering prizes to be won by those whose eyes were clear, and who kept their swords sharp and their courage high. Walter Raleigh was an Elizabethan adventurer.

The later Elizabethans were superbly self-confident. Their poise was unassailable. The generation before theirs had been harsh, treacherous, tenacious, adaptable. It had been moulded by the

[1] A. L. Rowse, *The England of Elizabeth I*, 110.

dangers of a time when religion was constantly changing and the ferment of the Renaissance and Reformation was frothing in its first fury. The men of that previous generation needed to be prudent to escape the sharp or fiery perils which brought many statesmen to the block, and many prelates to the stake. Not for nothing was the epithet ' foxy ' so frequently on men's lips during that period. Contemporary records are full of references to ' the foxy Gardiner', ' Bonner the fox', 'the old fox, Burghley'.

Men are moulded by the times in which they live, and it was Raleigh's fortune to live in an age during which the gentry—the class to which he belonged—rose for the first time to economic and social predominance. He was one of a new generation of uninhibited, brilliant, dashing, gay young men, whose supreme achievement, in the field of thought, was the Shakespearian drama, and, in the field of action, the expansion of England overseas and the colonization of North America.

The gentry had been rising slowly since the middle of the thirteenth century, but their numbers and influence increased on an unprecedented scale as the sixteenth century drew towards its close. Part of the old feudal nobility had been destroyed during the fifteenth century in the Wars of the Roses; and peers owned a far smaller proportionate amount of land during Elizabethan times than they had done under the Plantagenets or than they were to own later under the Hanoverians. Moreover the bishops, with the exceptions of London, Durham, Win-

chester, and the two archbishops, found themselves
reduced, after the Reformation, to a level with the
gentry.

By far the strongest impetus, however, to the
advancement of the landowning gentry was given
when Henry VIII dissolved the monasteries, chan-
tries, and guilds. Almost at a stroke about one-fifth
of all the available land in England and Wales
changed ownership and was tossed into the market
as a reward for the shrewd, the enterprising, the
ambitious, or the merely fortunate. That social
revolution offered the best and most exciting field
of opportunity since the Conquest. Some former
church property, naturally, went to those who had
leased it from or managed it for the monasteries.
But over the country as a whole between one-half
to two-thirds of that land was used to increase the
wealth and consequence of the dynamic class of
gentry which gave the nation the leadership that
it needed, and launched it into new paths at home
and overseas.

Throughout the later sixteenth century, improved
farming methods continued to provide increasingly
satisfactory yields. Men will always do more for
their own property than they will for that of others.
The overall pattern varied in different parts of the
country; in general, however, capital accumulated
rapidly and the rich grew constantly more prosperous. Many plain yeomen shared in that widespread
diffusion of prosperity, but as a result of enclosures
and rising prices the condition of the lower classes

often deteriorated. There were times when the roads swarmed with bands of uprooted vagabonds, and the problem of poor relief became a major preoccupation of government.

Prices rushed upwards throughout Western Europe from about the middle of the sixteenth century. The main cause was the import into Spain of treasure from the mines of Central and South America. The consequent diffusion of bullion inflated the currencies of all nations, and it is estimated that in England prices were trebled, on an average, between 1550 and 1650. Wages tended constantly to lag behind prices, but as capital became abundant England was quick to exploit her industrial, commercial, and geographical advantages. By the end of the sixteenth century she had already reached that position of economic supremacy which she retained until the end of the nineteenth century.

England possessed an abundance of natural products—corn, timber, coal, wool, iron—and, in the woollen industry, an immemorial tradition of manufacturing skill and commercial experience. There were no wars on English soil, no crippling tolls, and no settled caste divisions to impede social mobility. In those circumstances, the rate of industrial and commercial expansion in England was greater relatively during the lifeimes of Shakespeare and Raleigh than at any period before the end of the eighteenth century. An atmosphere of freedom helped to provide ideally responsive conditions when, during the second half of the sixteenth century, a wind of creative enterprise seemed to sweep across the land. No period could have been more stimulating, and Lord Keynes considered[1] that never in the annals of the modern world has there existed so prolonged and so rich an opportunity for the business man, the speculator, or the profiteer."

That view may be slightly exaggerated, and most people would probably hold that the nineteenth century provided even greater opportunities. The record of the earlier period is nevertheless extraordinarily impressive. The sixteenth century witnessed the break-up of a traditional economic and social order, and no people profited more than the English from the changed conditions. No person, moreover, in that age, exploited those new opportunities with greater gusto and over a wider field than Sir Walter Raleigh.

Self-reliance was the keynote in the lives of all the great Elizabethans. Their outlook was secular, and it reflected the intense and glowing experience of a people which had just attained maturity and emerged into the blinding sunlight and full summer of the English Renaissance. The Elizabethans were magnificent in their dress, behaviour, bearing, and manner of life; and that magnificence was perfectly illustrated by the way in which some of the great ministers and courtiers built prodigy houses, to the limit of their resources, and beyond, as an expression of their cult of sovereignty. Sir John Thynne, for

[1] Lord Keynes, *Treatise on Money*, 11, 159, quoted by A. L. Rowse, *The England of Elizabeth, I.* 109.

example, built Longleat—perhaps the loveliest of all historic English homes to-day—and William Cecil built Burghley and Theobalds, primarily as palaces for the reception of the Queen and Court during royal progresses through the country.

Of all the great Elizabethans, none was prouder, more self-confident, or more magnificent than Sir Walter Raleigh. He represented the ideal of Renaissance man, and he suffered to a quite unusual degree from the contemporary vice of intellectual pride. The restricted circumstances of his early years, his passionate ambition, and his resentment at the refusal of others to appreciate at his own valuation the superb gifts of which he was fully conscious, made him contemptuous of his fellows and careless of their feelings. He possessed genius, as well as the quality of magnetism which attracts and moves currents of opinion, and he was filled with a warm humanity which caused him to espouse the cause of the poor and the distressed. But the poor hated his arrogance, and the Court resented the complacency of one whose rise had been meteoric and whose origins were relatively obscure.

Raleigh never learned to guard his tongue, and his speculative mind caused him to be regarded as an atheist. That accusation was unjust, but the odium which it aroused contributed to his widespread unpopularity. Lack of caution was a weakness which he never overcame; it exposed him in 1603 to a charge of treason which led him, ultimately, to the block. He took little interest in points of doctrine or in controverted forms of worship, but his years of imprisonment in the Tower brought him back to the position—if he had ever consciously abandoned it—of a believing Christian.

Raleigh would never stoop to practise consistently the art of pleasing; and a mastery of that art was essential for success in the courtier's career which he deliberately adopted. He therefore made bitter enemies and failed even to begin to conciliate the intense jealousy which he provoked. He was not able to endure fools; he was quick to resent slights; yet he seldom hesitated to score off anyone, however eminent, whom he considered slower-witted or less brilliant than himself.

Those faults contributed to Raleigh's ruin, but such ruin does not necessarily imply failure. He was the finest prose-writer of his age, after Bacon; he was a good poet; he was a founder of Empire. He was happy to lose a fortune in pursuit of his darling plan for the colonization of North America. During his lifetime he was a glittering, romantic, and controversial figure, whose name was a household word. And that name has continued to dazzle and fascinate posterity.

* 1 *

' Say to the Court it Glows '

W̱ALTER RALEIGH was born at Hayes Barton, near Budleigh Salterton, in Devon. The year was probably 1554. His family was honourably regarded, but it had never been even locally power-ful. Raleigh's father, another Walter Raleigh, married three times; Walter was the second son of his father's third marriage, to Katherine Cham-pernown, widow of Otto Gilbert. Sir Humphrey Gilbert, the great sailor, was Raleigh's half-brother; as a child he had been a page to the Queen, and that connection with the Court was later to prove useful to Walter. Devon was at that time the cradle of English maritime adventure, and Raleigh was connected with many well-known sea-faring families. As a boy it was his great delight to question men of the sea, and to talk with them about their adventures in distant parts of the world.

Of his formal education little is known. He went up to Oriel College, Oxford, probably in 1568, at the age of eighteen, and he remained a student throughout his life. But he stayed little more than a year at the University. His spirit was too eager;

he longed for adventure; where he himself was concerned he was inclined always to take the short view in preference to the long. In 1569—the year of the rising of the Northern Earls—he joined a unit of mounted volunteers from Devon which was aiding the Huguenot cause in France. That unit was commanded by his cousin, Henry Champernown. In his *History of the World*, Raleigh casually mentions that he was present at the Battle of Montcontour (3rd October, 1569).

He seems to have stayed some six years in France, while his name remained on the books of Oriel College, but his experiences did not mature him to any great extent. In some respects he never did mature. On his return from France he took lodgings at Islington, and was entered as a student at the Middle Temple. He did not, however, study seriously, and when he was being tried for treason in 1603 he said he had never read a word of law. However, he made useful friends, and some complimentary verses by him were prefaced to George Gascoigne's *The Steel Glass*, which was published in 1576. Gascoigne was a social figure who had served in Flanders with Humphrey Gilbert. He was a popular poet during Shakespeare's boyhood, and Raleigh's earliest surviving poem contained four lines which forecast with pathetic clarity what was to be his own fate:

> *But envious brains do nought, or light, esteem*
> *Such stately steps as they cannot attain.*

For whoso reaps renown above the rest
With heaps of hate shall surely be oppressed.

Many of Raleigh's friends at that period were
what Aubrey called ' boisterous blades, but generally those that had wit '. He was brilliant, flashy,
quarrelsome, and frustrated. On one occasion he
was confined for six days in the Fleet prison for his
part in a brawl, and afterwards bound over to keep
the peace. On another, it is on record that growing
angry at a tavern with one of his companions who
was ' a perpetual talker, and made a noise like a
drum in a room ', he sealed up the offender's
mouth with wax.

Still, the need to earn a living remained. To a
youth of Raleigh's spirit and versatility it was a
small matter to shift his interest from soldiering to
the sea. Humphrey Gilbert had done the same;
he had been knighted in 1570 for his services in
helping to suppress a rebellion in Ireland, and had
later helped the rebels in the Netherlands who had
risen against Philip II of Spain. By 1573 he had
concentrated his interest on America, and after
writing numerous petitions, he was granted a patent
to organize an expedition to the New World.
Raleigh joined in that venture; it was the first of
a very large number with which he was to be
intimately associated throughout his life. Such
expeditions were run on a joint-stock basis, and
anyone could take a share in them. Elizabeth
herself often took shares.

After sundry mishaps, including a quarrel with a Seville merchant whose ship and cargo of oranges and lemons Gilbert and Raleigh seized at Dartmouth and were ordered to restore, an expedition consisting of seven ships and 150 men sailed from Plymouth on 18th November, 1579. Raleigh commanded one of the vessels, but the flotilla ran into a superior Spanish force off Cape Verde, and an action was fought. The English ships scattered, and all, except one which was lost, eventually made their ways back to Plymouth. Raleigh arrived late with his provisions almost exhausted. His first naval venture, like his last, ended in failure.

Open war between England and Spain did not begin until 1588, but the intense bitterness and rivalry which divided the two peoples often flared previously into acts of hostility all over the globe. At bottom the cause was economic, but in contemporary thought the religious issue crystallized the new division of mankind, and caused Europe to pass through a fiery furnace before cooling at long last into what was to be its eighteenth-century shape. Spain directed the Counter-Reformation which had been organized by a reformed papacy; she was resolved to exclude all foreigners from the New World and from the newly-discovered shores of Asia and Africa, and she was in the habit of handing over English sailors and merchants to the Inquisition. She had no thought of tolerating indefinitely an England permanently severed from the Roman Catholic communion.

England, on the other hand, was discovering that its former remote position on the edge of the known world had ' changed into a central point of vantage dominating the modern routes of trade and colonization; and that power, wealth, and adventure lay for Englishmen at the far end of ocean voyages fabulously long ', leading to Africa, Asia, and the half-empty colony of America, ' which was piecing itself together year by year under the astonished eyes of men, upsetting all known ideas of cosmogony and all customs of commerce '.[1]   In seeking out those distant markets, the rising class of English capitalists was partly tempted by the rich rewards to be earned, and partly spurred by necessity owing to the closing of old routes and markets nearer home. The expansion of overseas enterprise and, above all, the colonization of North America, constituted the height of Raleigh's ambition throughout his life; English merchants and seamen, acting on their own initiative, but with the connivance and sympathy of their Government, were determined that no power on earth should stop them from sharing in the wealth and commerce of the New World.   The growing Protestant sentiment of the English people provided what would to-day be called an ideology opposed to that of the Spanish Catholic Empire.

In the British Isles at that time the principal danger-point was Ireland, where Jesuit missionaries, Franciscans, and priests trained at Irish colleges newly established at Douai and Salamanca, were

[1] G. M. Trevelyan, *History of England*, 338.

kindling a fanatical spirit of revolt against the
heretic Queen and English misrule. It was to
Ireland that Raleigh turned next in pursuit of fame
and fortune. The old system of aristocratic home
rule through the great Anglo-Irish families had
come to an end. No other system had taken its
place, and the arbitrary, vacillating, hand-to-mouth,
absentee English Government was accompanied by
every species of corruption and exploitation. As
the quarrel between England and Spain became
more inflamed, the danger to England from her
Achilles heel in Ireland grew steadily greater. Compelled most reluctantly to undertake the conquest
of Ireland, England's conduct of the campaign was
stained by terrible cruelties in which Raleigh was
about to play a full part.

Captain Raleigh obtained his commission through
friends at Court, and that fact is less strange than it
might at first glance appear. The Court, like a great
magnet, attracted all who were ambitious to shine
and cut a great figure. The English gentry had
long been noted for their habit of turning younger
sons out of the manor-house and into the rough
world to push their fortunes. It was, therefore,
inevitable that means should exist whereby youths
of spirit should have a chance of winning a place in
the sun.

During Elizabeth's reign an obvious and promis-
ing method was to enlist the patronage of some
established Court favourite; to become useful and,
if possible, indispensable to him; and to be rewarded

subsequently with opportunities of elbowing a path to the front. During Raleigh's boyhood an unusually large number of obscure but ambitious younger sons had attached themselves to Elizabeth's reigning favourite, Robert Dudley, Earl of Leicester, and Raleigh was numbered among those. Raleigh's half-brother, Sir Humphrey Gilbert, who had once been a page to the Queen, had worked a good deal with Leicester and was on good terms with Sir Francis Walsingham, the Secretary of State. Through Gilbert, Raleigh was able to approach Walsingham at an early stage in his career, and he owed his commission to those important and valuable connections. He resolved to make himself conspicuous within the shortest possible time.

Raleigh landed at Cork in August, 1580, in command of a ' footband ' of one hundred men from London, and was plunged at once into a campaign to suppress a dangerous rising which had broken out in Munster, the Fitzgerald country. Spanish and papal aid was expected by the rebels, and Lord Grey de Wilton, the Lord Deputy of Ireland, had orders to crush the rising. Raleigh came under command of General the Earl of Ormonde, and one of his first assignments was to sit on a court-martial which tried Sir James Fitzgerald, brother of the Earl of Desmond. Sir James was sentenced to be hanged, drawn, and quartered, and that sentence was carried out.

The war was an affair of besieged castles, massacred garrisons, and a scorched-earth policy applied

by the English to the rebel countryside. Pitched
battles were rare events. Raleigh became expert at
guerrilla warfare; his feats of bravery became a
legend, and were soon celebrated far and wide. He
was merciless and fearless. A typical episode was
his arrest of Lord Roche, an Anglo-Irish magnate
who was suspect to the authorities. Riding from
the headquarters at Cork through hostile country by
night, with a force of ninety men, Captain Raleigh
disposed them about Roche's stronghold. He then
marched to the entrance and demanded its surrender. Five hundred of Roche's armed followers
were drawn up in defence of their chief, and a parley
followed. Raleigh secured permission to enter with
three companions in order to discuss the situation
over breakfast with his host. However, by a clever
ruse, he succeeded in securing an entry for his
entire force. He immediately seized Lord Roche
and threatened to cut his throat if any attempt were
made to stop him marching his captive back to
Cork. The next night he marched through a
countryside which had been roused against him; but
he evaded his enemies, and returned in triumph
with his prisoner. It is pleasant to record that Lord
Roche succeeded later in clearing himself.

The foreign aid which the Pope and King Philip
had promised took the form of a force, some hun-
dreds strong, officered mainly by Italians, and liber-
ally supplied with arms to assist the rebellion. The
invaders made an ancient fort in the Bay of Smer-
wick their headquarters, and there, in November,

1580, they were besieged by land and blockaded by sea. At first they refused to surrender, but, after a violent bombardment lasting two days, they asked for terms. None were offered, and the invaders surrendered at discretion. Captains Raleigh and Mackworth were sent in to clean up the situation. The officers, numbering twenty, were set on one side, for ransom. Of the rest, the Irish, men and women, were hanged, and the foreigners put to the sword. Lord Grey, who was commanding in person, reported that Raleigh and Mackworth fell straight to execution, so that 600 stripped bodies 'as gallant and goodly personages as ever were beheld' were presently laid out on the sand.

That was not a pretty business, but the poet, Edmund Spenser, who was Grey's secretary and later became Raleigh's intimate friend, did his best to ward off the charge of cruelty. The Irish, he wrote, 'were no lawful enemies, but rebels and traitors; and therefore they that came to succour them, no better than rogues and renegades'. Guerrilla warfare has always aroused the basest instincts; in his book, *A View of the Present State of Ireland*, the sensitive Spenser painted many pictures of the horrors of that campaign. Of the state to which Munster was reduced he wrote:

'For notwithstanding that the same was a most rich and plentiful country, full of corn and cattle, so that you would have thought they would have been able to stand long, yet, ere one year and a half they were brought to such wretchedness, as

that any stony heart would have rued the same.
Out of every corner of the woods and glens they came
creeping forth upon their hands, for their legs
could not bear them; they looked like anatomies of
death; they spake like ghosts crying out of their
graves; they did eat of the dead carrions; happy
were they if they could find them; yea, and one
another soon after, insomuch as the very carcasses
they spared not to scrape out of their graves . . .'

And again, more specifically, writing of the execution of a ' notable traitor ' at Limerick:

' I saw an old woman, which was his foster-mother,
take up his head, whilst he was quartered, and sucked
up all the blood running thereout, saying that the
earth was not worthy to drink it, and therewith also
steeped her face and breast, and tore her hair,
crying out and shrieking out most terribly.'

By horrors of that kind Raleigh was unmoved.
His principal concern was to see the devastated
countryside repopulated by loyal sons of Devon,
after their commanders had been suitably rewarded
by grants of confiscated land. He petitioned himself
for the grant of an alleged rebel property near Cork,
and found Walsingham sympathetic. But Burghley
intervened so that Raleigh, on that occasion, was
disappointed.

For the present he had to be content to use the
goodwill he had earned by his reckless courage and
success in the field to intrigue against his chiefs with
the authorities at home. He complained of their
incompetence and lack of severity in dealing with

the Irish. The rules of subordination were not at
that period strictly enforced, but the tactlessness
and want of scruple shown by Raleigh was one cause
of the distrust and dislike that he came to inspire
in many quarters. It is impossible to ignore that.
He wrote to Walsingham on 25th February, 1581,
to complain about the mismanagement of the war,
and about the conduct of his commander, Lord
Ormonde.

' Would God your Honour and Her Majesty as
well as my poor self, understood how pitifully the
service here goeth forward! Considering that this
man, having been Lord General of Munster now
about two years, there are at this instant a thousand
traitors more than there were the first day.'

He went on to contrast Ormonde unfavourably
with Sir Humphrey Gilbert, ' who with the third
part of the garrison now in Ireland, ended a rebellion not much inferior to this, in two months! '
On 25th August, 1581, he wrote with characteristic
arrogance to Lord Leicester, to complain that he
had been forgotten:

' Your Honour, having no use of such poor followers, hath utterly forgotten me. . . . I have spent
some time here under the Deputy, in such poor
place and charge as, were it not that I knew him
to be one of yours, I would disdain it as much as to
keep sheep.' He went on to describe Ireland as
a ' lost land '—not a ' commonwealth ', but a
common woe '.

Raleigh was on the make; he was fretting for a

more profitable employment. He was a very difficult subordinate, and when his unit was disbanded
in December, 1581, his chiefs must have been glad
to see him go. He was the bearer of despatches to
London. That was his reward and the opportunity
which he was quick to seize. He already possessed
some interest at Court where his reputation for
gallantry and dare-devilry had preceded him.
Everything depended upon the impression which he
was able to make upon the Queen; and that impression could hardly have been more favourable. His
reception was extremely gracious and it proved
to be the turning-point in his life. His fine presence
enchanted Elizabeth. His West Country burr
intrigued her. His ready tongue and strong personality were additional recommendations, and she
took him, it was said, ' for a kind of oracle, which
nettled them all '. Walter Raleigh had arrived.

Many stories were told of his growing intimacy
with the Queen. Walking with her one day at
Greenwich, they came to a ' plashy ' place. Raleigh
immediately whipped off his rich cloak and flung
it down over the mud, so that the Queen might
pass dryshod. That famous incident is so much in
character that there is no reason to cast doubt on it.
On another occasion he is said to have scratched
with a diamond upon a window some words which
were intended to attract the Queen's eye:

　　' Fain would I rise, yet fear I to fall.'
The Queen, in reply, is said to have scratched the
words:

' If thy heart fail thee, rise not at all.'
It was commonly believed that when he first arrived in London, Raleigh's clothes formed the best part of his estate. He took immense pains with his dress, and his jewels and lace were celebrated. Raleigh constantly discussed Irish affairs with the Queen and her ministers, and on 1st January, 1582, the Lord Deputy, Grey, wrote reproachfully to Burghley:

' When it shall have come under your Lordship's deeper consideration, I doubt not but you will soon discern a difference between the judgments of those which, with grounded experience and approved reason, look into the condition of things, and those which, upon no ground but seeming fancies and affecting credit with profit, frame " plots " upon impossibilities for others to execute.'

The particular ' plot ' to which Grey was referring was a plan drawn up by Raleigh and presented by him to the Queen, for the better conduct of the war in Munster. It was at first intended that Raleigh should return to Ireland, with a new command. When Grey was notified of that by Walsingham, on 2nd April, 1582, he replied indignantly:

' For mine own part, I must be plain: I like neither his carriage nor his company; and therefore, other than by direction and commandment, and what his right can require, he is not to expect at my hands.'

It is hard not to sympathize with Grey, but Elizabeth began to have other ideas for her new favourite. She employed his services herself, and

sent him on Leicester's staff on a mission to the
Low Countries, where he met William the Silent,
Prince of Orange, and the Duc d'Alençon, Elizabeth's
pertinacious suitor. The mission was of short dura-
tion, but the Queen had missed him during his
absence, and on his return his rise was rapid and
spectacular.

II

All Elizabeth's favourites were given nicknames
by their Sovereign, and she made a free use of
Christian names to others. ' She intoxicated Court
and country, and keyed her realm to the intensity
of her own spirit ';[1] the Court was kept in a state
of perpetual effervescence. Leicester was her
' Eyes ', or, alternatively, her ' sweet Robyn '. He
used to embellish his letters to her with a pair of
eyes. Christopher Hatton, her mouthpiece in the
House of Commons, and, later, Lord Chancellor,
was her ' Lids ', her ' Mutton ', or her ' Bell-
Wether '. The swarthy Walsingham was her
' Moor '; Burghley her ' Spirit '; Raleigh was
nicknamed ' Water '. The romantic conventions of
the age, and the intimate way in which the Sovereign wrote and spoke to the inner circle of her
Court, gave rise to malicious gossip in the outer
circle. That gossip has reverberated from age to
age, but there is no substance behind it—not a tittle
of evidence to support it.

[1] J. E. Neale, *Queen Elizabeth*, 215.

Evidence accumulated swiftly, however, of Raleigh's growing consequence. In April, 1583, All Souls College, Oxford, was induced to assign him the leases of two properties. In the following month, the great Burghley regarded the favourite as so firmly established that he begged him to intercede with the Queen on behalf of his son-in-law, the Earl of Oxford, who had been involved in a duel. Raleigh did as he was asked, but, characteristically, he did it with a bad grace, making it plain that he had no love for Lord Oxford.

In the years which immediately followed, Raleigh was the recipient of licences, commercial monopolies, and estates which made him a very wealthy man, and gave him, as such, a standing in the country. In 1583 he was granted a patent for the 'Farm of Wines', which required every vintner in the Kingdom to pay him one pound a year in return for his licence. He had a hot dispute with Cambridge University over the terms of his patent, and both Universities established their right to remain outside its terms. The patent was worth about a thousand pounds a year—a big sum at that time; he was also given a licence to export woollen broadcloth. In July, 1585, he became Lord Warden of the Stannaries, a lucrative office which, besides other duties, gave him command of the militia in Devon and Cornwall—a force ten to thirteen thousand strong. He also enjoyed monopolies for the sale of tin, and playing-cards. He was appointed Lord-Lieutenant of Cornwall, and Vice-Admiral of Cornwall and

Devon. He became one of Devon's two M.P.s in
1584, and was knighted. It was, however, his grants
of lands and property which afford the most impressive evidence of Elizabeth's regard. As early as
1584 he was in a position to buy his birthplace at
Hayes Barton, and to announce, characteristically,
that ' being born in that house, I had rather seat
myself there than any where else '. But his ideas
expanded rapidly. In the devastated province of
Munster alone he acquired 40,000 acres, including
Lismore Castle; he set to work immediately to
plant that vast domain with loyal sons of Devon.
In 1586, after the failure of Anthony Babington's
plot to assassinate the Queen, the greater part of
that unhappy traitor's estates in five Midland
counties were tossed, as a free gift, to Raleigh. He
was relieved of paying any fees when the Great Seal
was attached to the grant. In order that the favourite might have a suitable London residence in
which to maintain his dazzling position, Durham
Palace, in the Strand, was alienated from the See of
Durham and assigned to Raleigh. Aubrey provided a pen-picture of Raleigh living there ' after
he came to his greatness ':

' I well remember his study, which was a little
turret that looked into and over the Thames, and
had the prospect which is pleasant, perhaps, as
any in the world, and which not only refreshes
the eyesight but cheers the spirits, and (to speak
my mind) I believe enlarges an ingenious man's
thoughts.'

HUMFRIDUS GILBERTUS EQ AURATUS MILES

Quid Non

GILBETUS ciues alium deduxit in orbem
Quó CHRISTI imbuerit barbara corda fide AB

Plate 1 Sir Humphrey Gilbert

Plate 2 Robert Dudley, Earl of Leicester, by an unknown artist

To that turret, which Lady Raleigh in later years detested, were invited the intimate friends with whom Raleigh liked best to live—the poets Spenser and Marlowe, Hariot the scientist, Hooker the ecclesiastical writer, and Hakluyt, whose *Voyages* did so much to concentrate and dramatize his countrymen's interest in maritime adventure and exploration. By dedications and in other ways Hakluyt was lavish in his praise of Raleigh and in his acknowledgment of indebtedness to him.

Of all the grants which Raleigh received, none gave him quite so much satisfaction as that of the Manor of Sherborne, in Dorsetshire, with its ancient town and abbey. Elizabeth persuaded the Bishop and Chapter of Salisbury to lease that property to her so that she might assign it to Raleigh in January, 1592. Raleigh rounded the property off by buying Wilscombe Manor from the Bishop of Bath, but it was at Sherborne that he always felt most completely at home. He restored and improved the house with loving care; he indulged in the delights of building; he planted trees and laid out gardens, and when all the rest of his world was tumbling into ruins about his head, it was Sherborne he tried hardest, but in vain, to preserve from the wreck of his fortunes.

None of the offices to which Raleigh was appointed suited him so well as that of Captain of the Yeomen of the Guard; he was appointed in 1586 at the age of 34. The Guard, which consisted of 50 chosen youths, was responsible day and night for

the Queen's personal safety. Aubrey had a good
story about Raleigh's conduct in that office:

' There came a country gentleman (or sufficient
yeoman) up to Town, who had several sons, but
one an extraordinary proper, handsome fellow,
whom he did hope to have preferred to be a Yeoman
of the Guard. The father (a goodly man himself)
comes to Sir Walter Raleigh, a stranger to him, and
told him that he had brought up a boy that he would
desire (having many children) should be one of
Her Majesty's Guard. Quoth Sir Walter Raleigh,
" Had you spake for yourself I should readily have
granted your desire, for your person deserves it, but
I put in no boys." Said his father, " Boy, come in."
The Son enters, at about 18 or 19, but such a goodly
proper young Fellow as Sir Walter had not seen
the like: He was the tallest of all the Guard. Sir
Walter swears him immediately; and ordered him
to carry up the first Dish at Dinner, when the Queen
beheld him with admiration, as if a beautiful young
Giant had stalked in with the service.'

By tradition, the Captain of the Guard could
aspire to the highest offices in the Kingdom, but
Raleigh achieved none of them. He was regarded
as an upstart and hated for his pride, and he never
attempted to do anything to conciliate that feeling.
Sir Anthony Bagot, in 1587, called him ' the best
hated man in Court, city, and country '. That
would not, perhaps, have mattered greatly if he
had been able to discipline his nature to an extent
sufficient to enable him to make a more solid and

effective contribution to the State's service. The Queen made him work hard, but he dissipated his energies, for the most part, on raiding expeditions which sometimes cost more to organize than they achieved in booty collected, in schemes of colonization and exploration which served his country only in the long run and were regarded as whimsical by his contemporaries, and in improvements to his various properties.

In the days of his greatness, money ran through Raleigh's fingers like water. He sank no less than forty thousand pounds—a princely fortune in those days—in his colonization plans. On the other hand he scorned a profit of a mere one hundred per cent on a raiding expedition, and remarked on one occasion in his lordly way that he would have done better to have sent his warships fishing. He was generous as well as extravagant; he patronized learning; but too much of his wealth found its way into the pockets of dishonest underlings, or was wasted on personal display. In one sense Raleigh never seemed to grow up, and his clothes became so gorgeous as to cause even that brilliant Court to smile. He blazed with diamonds, rubies, and pearls. The Flemish Jesuit, Drexelius, estimated that the jewels he wore on his shoes alone were worth six thousand six hundred gold pieces.

It is true, as Aubrey says, that Raleigh was ' no slug '. He possessed immense vitality; he loved magnificence; and he spent on a fantastic scale. But he relied too much on his fine figure and ready tongue to bring him those rewards which other men were content to acquire through more usual channels. The subtle Elizabeth soon discerned his weakness. She relished his magnetism and his robust ways, and she was thrilled by his brilliance and versatility; but she doubted his statesmanship and discretion. She never made him a Privy Councillor and she gave him no command in the great crisis when the Spanish Armada put to sea. Until he fell temporarily from favour, at the age of forty, in 1592, Raleigh lived on the promise of his youth. He had never laid his foundations deep in public opinion, and they were liable to be upset by a breath of wind. When the boy Essex, with the historic name, soft, dreamy eyes, small hands, tall figure, high spirits, and hair the colour of ripe corn, appeared at Court in 1587, aged only twenty, Raleigh's position was seriously shaken. It was no answer to provoke Essex to a duel. Essex became the author of his own destruction, but, later, a new age arose which took a different and more prosaic view of the privateering business in which Raleigh had specialized all his life. When that happened he was completely overturned.

★ 2 ★

Public Life

THERE IS a well-known passage in the *History of the Peloponnesian War*, in which Thucydides, who flourished in the fifth century before Christ, pointed out that in early times the profession of pirate was held in high repute:

'An illustration of this', he wrote, 'is furnished by the honour with which some of the inhabitants of the Continent still regard a successful marauder, and by the question we find the old poets everywhere representing the people as asking of voyagers —" Are they pirates? "—as if it implied no reproach, and as if those to whom it was put would not disclaim such an occupation.' [1]

Those conditions were roughly paralleled in the dawn of Europe's colonization of the New World. Drake, Hawkins, Gilbert, Grenville, and Raleigh were all professional pirates whose activities were approved and held, for a time, in high respect by their fellow-countrymen. But, on a long view, the ends Raleigh had in mind were more creative than those of his colleagues. He was no specialist, and

[1] Translated by Sir Richard Livingstone.

35

in no sense a professional sailor as were Drake, Grenville, and Hawkins. His outlook was much broader and less cruel. Raleigh's place in the long and glorious line of British admirals is secure and honourable; it is, however, that of a lifelong amateur. He grew soft at Court during the 1580s, but he made ample amends during the next decade. He counted on making a huge fortune out of privateering, and on using it to finance his project of planting a new England on the other side of the ocean. That, throughout his life, remained his dearest ambition.

By using his influence with the Queen, Raleigh secured permission for Sir Humphrey Gilbert to sail to North America in June, 1583, in command of a small expedition of five ships with a view to founding a colony. Raleigh had hoped himself to serve as Gilbert's Vice-Admiral, but the Queen could not bring herself to let him go. He spent a large sum on a 200-ton vessel—the *Bark Raleigh*— which he supplied for the expedition, but the voyage ended in disaster. Four ships reached Newfoundland, and only one regained Plymouth. All the rest were lost, including the Admiral, Sir Humphrey Gilbert. The final disaster has become an epic of the sea. When two vessels only remained, Gilbert transferred his flag from the larger, which displaced forty tons, to the smaller, which displaced no more than ten. A storm arose, and when Sir Humphrey was last hailed, he was sitting abaft with a book in his hand, and was heard to cry out:

' We are as near to Heaven by sea, as by land! '

No time was wasted in repining. Raleigh set to work at once to organize a new venture. It is the one for which he is best remembered. He secured, in 1584, a patent to colonize Virginia, a name which the Queen graciously allowed to be applied to a vast, unmapped, undefined territory in North America. A small preliminary expedition of two ships was sent to spy out the land, and it reported very favourably on the soil, climate, and natives.

Raleigh's patent gave him and his heirs full proprietary rights, subject to certain reservations. Philip II's agent in Paris (he had formerly been ambassador in London) reported to his master that the Queen, after knighting Raleigh, had promised to pay all the expenses of the expedition on condition that he would not risk his life by accompanying it. The expedition of seven ships sailed on 9th April, 1585, and was commanded by Sir Richard Grenville who took Raleigh's place.

Raleigh remained behind, but he sent with the expedition Thomas Cavendish, the second Englishman to circumnavigate the globe, and John White, the cartographer, and the earliest of our watercolour artists. He also sent his friend, Thomas Hariot, a distinguished Oxford mathematician and astronomer. Raleigh had become intimate with Hariot some years earlier, and had learnt mathematics from him. They remained friends as long as they both lived, and Hariot was with Raleigh on the night before his execution.

Hariot made many discoveries in algebra, pure mathematics, and astronomy, but as he refrained from publishing his results, others gained the credit for them. On the expedition to Virginia, however, Hariot served Raleigh in the office of geographer, and his *Brief & True Report of the Land of Virginia* was duly published in 1588. It was an admirable and comprehensive survey of the country which it described, and it was reprinted in Hakluyt's *Voyages*. It provided Raleigh with excellent publicity material and he made full use of it.

After a little privateering on the way, the expedition reached Roanoke Island (North Carolina) successfully, and 107 men were landed under the governorship of John Lane. Grenville sailed off to enjoy some profitable piracy on the Spanish Main, while Raleigh busied himself with arrangements for supplies and reinforcements. Unhappily, trouble arose with the natives, and when Drake suddenly appeared in command of a sizeable fleet, the colonists' morale was low. Drake was in an amiable mood after sacking a number of Spanish towns and taking some valuable prizes. Finding the colonists completely disheartened, he provided them with a ship of 170 tons displacement, in which they, and Hariot, sailed home. Raleigh's relief expedition arrived a day or two after they had left, and Grenville returned a little later with more supplies. Understanding how disappointed Raleigh would be, he landed fifteen volunteer colonists of his own to keep the settlement alive.

When his original colonists arrived home, Raleigh at once set to work to organize a further expedition. He, too, had been enjoying a run of good fortune with his privateering enterprises; two of his ships had secured some particularly valuable prizes off the Azores, and he used the proceeds to collect another 117 colonists and to organize an expedition of three ships to transport them. They sailed on 8th May, 1587, under John White, but one ship turned back in the Bay of Biscay. The other two reached Roanoke Island to discover that Grenville's fifteen volunteers had been murdered by the natives. That melancholy event discouraged White's party of 100 men and seventeen women. John White's daughter, Eleanor, wife of Ananias Dare, gave birth to the first European baby to be born on American soil. She was christened, appropriately, Virginia.

Relations with the natives soon grew precarious, and White allowed himself to be persuaded to return to England in one of the ships which had brought them out, in order to impress on Raleigh the need for haste in supplying reinforcements and provisions. But he arrived home at a bad time. All available shipping was being held against the threat of Spanish invasion. It was only with great difficulty that Raleigh secured permission to fulfil his promises to the colonists. But the two ships he despatched were turned back by French pirates, and the colonists were left to their fate.

Raleigh had already spent huge sums on his venture. It would, as Hakluyt said, ' have re-

quired a prince's purse to have followed out ' what
he had begun. In March, 1589, therefore, Raleigh
handed over his patent to a company of London
merchants, but his interest in his colony never
flagged. After White had sailed for Roanoke Island,
and failed to find his flock—it had moved to another
island—Raleigh sent out five further expeditions in
thirteen years. He talked and wrote about his colony
continuously, but it was to no purpose. The natives
had destroyed it, and only a few pathetic traces of
it were discovered.

Raleigh's venture in Virginia failed, but in the
long perspective of history his abortive efforts to
found a New England in North America have an
honourable, perhaps an inevitable, place: ' I shall
yet live to see it an English nation ', he wrote to
Robert Cecil in 1602. He did not live to see that
prediction fulfilled. But nearly two centuries later,
in 1788, when the Convention of North Carolina
chose a site for its Seat of Government, it decreed
that it should be named Raleigh, after the great-
hearted Englishman who had had the vision to
descry the future across the mists of ocean and the
years.

Before America could be effectively colonized it
was important that the colonists should discover
some permanent and distinctive economic resource.
Early in the seventeenth century that resource was
discovered in the tobacco plant, for which the soil
and climate of Virginia are ideally suited. Thomas
Hariot, in his *Brief & True Report*, had made strong

claims for the medicinal and other advantages of the habit of smoking. The first sizeable shipment of Virginian tobacco to England was made in 1614, while Raleigh was imprisoned in the Tower of London. It became the great staple commodity among the earliest settlers. It seems probable that tobacco was in fact first introduced into England by Sir John Hawkins, in 1566, but it is one further example of the magnetism of Raleigh's personality and of his unparalleled versatility that he should always have been popularly credited with having introduced the smoking habit into England. In one important sense the credit certainly is due to him, for he did more than anyone else to make that habit fashionable.

By the end of the sixteenth century smoking had become so general among all classes that tobacco was regarded as a socially necessary article of common consumption. It was one of the most widespread of the new luxuries of the age. During the seventeenth century tobacco became the principal source of the national revenue, and it has played ever since a vital role in economic and fiscal history. In 1954, for example, customs and excise receipts from tobacco amounted to no less than £626,810,000, compared with £278,845,000 from hydro-carbon oils and £242,032,000 excise receipts from beer, which are to-day the two next most profitable commodities from the standpoint of the Chancellor of the Exchequer.

Raleigh's long silver pipes and massive gold

tobacco-box became famous during his lifetime. There were numerous stories about his love for the weed. It was said, for example, that a new servant, when he first saw smoke issuing from his master's mouth and nostrils, ran at once to pour a bucket of water over Raleigh's head. The Queen on one occasion made a wisecrack which delighted Raleigh, for he loved to set the fashion and to hear his name on men's lips. The Queen said that she knew many who had turned gold into smoke, but that Raleigh was a true alchemist and the first, in her experience, who had succeeded in turning smoke into gold. It amused Raleigh to finger his pipes and to blow clouds of smoke into the faces of his traducers, but he could not have foreseen the tremendous importance of the part which the luxury he had popularized was to play in later economic and commercial history. He could not have foreseen also the immense influence he was destined to exert over the history of one particular nation, Ireland, by his well-known action in fostering upon his Irish properties, the cultivation of potatoes imported from the New World. It would be hard to exaggerate the importance of the part played by the potato in Irish economic history.

For the colonization of North America represented one side only of Raleigh's efforts to plant colonies of Englishmen overseas. The other side was represented by his effort to plant his large Irish properties with tenants and labourers from the West Country which he loved so well. He had two main resi-

dences in Ireland—Lismore Castle, which he started
to rebuild, and Youghal Manor. Besides planting
potatoes, he formed plans on both properties for
exporting timber to France and Spain to make
hogsheads. He failed, in the end, to obtain a
licence for that trade, but his Irish estates were
noted for being extremely well managed.

The year 1588 was overshadowed by the great
crisis of the Spanish Armada, which was first sighted
off the coast of Cornwall on 20th July. Raleigh was
given no command in the running battle which
followed as the Spaniards sailed up the Channel,
but the English Commander, Lord Howard of
Effingham, flew his flag in the *Ark Royal*, a vessel
which Raleigh had built and equipped. Raleigh
had to be content with organizing the militia in the
West of England for service in case the Spaniards
should succeed in effecting a landing.

After the Armada had passed Plymouth, the
danger of an invasion of the West Country appeared
to be at an end; Raleigh, accordingly, left his headquarters in Portland Castle and rushed up to
London. He begged to be allowed to join the fleet
in any humble capacity in its task of completing the
destruction of the Spanish fleet. The Armada was
at that time in trouble off Gravelines and Dunkirk,
and Raleigh was sent down with a message of
encouragement from the Queen to Lord Howard,
and with an order that the Spanish ships should be
engaged and sunk at all hazards if the fireships
failed to do their work.

After the defeat of the Armada, Raleigh resumed
his familiar work of organizing raiding expeditions;
but he was interrupted, during the summer of 1589,
by a momentary spell of the Royal displeasure. He
became involved in an intense struggle with Lord
Essex for the Queen's favour after the death of Lord
Leicester during the autumn of 1588.

When Essex, who was distantly related to the
Queen, arrived at Court in 1587 in the flower of his
youthful beauty, after signally distinguishing himself
in the mad charge of Zutphen, when Sir Philip
Sidney was killed, Elizabeth became infatuated
with him:

'Nobody with her,' wrote Sir Anthony Bagot
(May, 1887) 'but my Lord Essex; and at night my
Lord is at cards, or one game or another with her,
till the birds sing in the morning.'

Raleigh became jealous and alarmed, and Essex
was childishly intolerant of the older favourite.
The Queen scolded him and said that there was no
reason why he should 'disdain' Raleigh. She
laughed at him when he started to attack Raleigh
on the score of his low birth. Writing to a close
friend, Edward Dyer, a diplomat and poet, Essex
said that he had warned the Queen that Raleigh
was a knave:

'I did describe unto her what he has been and
what he was.'

As the Queen continued to defend her elder
favourite, Essex raised his voice, so that Raleigh,
who, as Captain of the Guard, was standing near

the door, would hear what he said. He stated that he told the Queen:

' I had no joy to be in any place, but was loth to be near about her, when I knew my affection so much thrown down, and such a wretch as Raleigh highly esteemed of her . . .'

That absurd arrogance was tiresome; but Essex fascinated the Queen so strongly that his enmity was dangerous. In the autumn of 1588 a duel was arranged between the rivals, but the Privy Council prevented it, and tried to stop any rumour of the affair from reaching the ears of the Queen. In the following year Essex, contrary to the Queen's orders, slipped off to join an abortive expedition, commanded by Drake and Norris, against Lisbon, while Raleigh left the Court to visit his Irish properties.

The ascendancy which Essex had gained over the Queen is proved by the ease with which he regained her favour after his return from Lisbon; it was generally believed that he was responsible for Raleigh's temporary retirement from the Court. Sir Francis Allen wrote to Anthony Bacon on 17 August, 1589:

' My Lord of Essex hath chased Mr. (*sic*) Raleigh from the Court and hath confined him into Ireland.'

It was evident that Raleigh was temporarily under a cloud, although he strenuously denied it. It is significant that he failed at that time in an attempt to obtain the Rangership of the New Forest for the Earl of Pembroke. The Queen gave it instead to Charles Blount, another of her handsome boys, who

actually fought a duel with Essex and became afterwards his devoted admirer.   Raleigh was in trouble
also over some of his privateering activities.   He had
seized a Flemish ship and was ordered to set it free.
He obeyed very grudgingly.   Such people, he protested, were merely ' Spaniards in disguise '.

The Lord Deputy of Ireland, Sir William Fitz-
william, made it plain by his manner that he considered that the favourite had stumbled.   Raleigh
wrote indignantly to his cousin, Sir George Carew
(afterwards Earl of Totnes):
'Cousin George,

' For my retreat from Court, it was upon good
cause to take order for my prize.   If in Ireland they
think I am not worth respecting they shall much
deceive themselves.   I am in place not to be believed inferior to any man, to pleasure or displeasure
the greatest;   and my opinion is so received and
believed as I can anger the best of them.'

He went on to assert, rather self-consciously, that
he considered himself of greater account than Fitz-
william in every way, and he ended characteristically:

' Farewell, noble George, my chosen friend and
kinsman, from whom nor time, nor fortune, nor
adversity shall ever sever me.'

II

It was during that visit to Ireland that Raleigh
became intimate with Edmund Spenser, his neigh-

Plate 3 Queen Elizabeth. Attributed to M. Gheeraedts

RIHARDVS GRENVILVS

Mil. aur.

Neptuni proles qui magni Martis alumñ
GRENVILIVS patrias sanguine tinxit aquas

Plate 4 Sir Richard Grenville

bour, who lived at Kilcolman Castle. That residence, together with 3,000 acres of land, had been
bestowed upon the poet as a reward for his services
during the Fitzgerald rebellion. Spenser and
Raleigh were both then aged thirty-seven; both
disliked the devastation by which they were surrounded in Munster; both delighted in poetry, and
found relief in composing it. Spenser was engaged
on his masterpiece, ' Faerie Queene,' when Raleigh
called to see him; and the resulting friendship
was celebrated by Spenser in a charming poem,
' Colin Clout's Come Home Again.' Spenser
described how Raleigh, to whom the poem was
dedicated, encouraged his work on ' Faerie Queene.'
He dubbed Raleigh ' The Shepherd of the Ocean ',
and explained how, while he (Spenser) was, in the
true pastoral tradition, keeping his sheep in the
cooling shade by Mulla's shore:

There a strange shepherd chanc'd to find me out,
  Whether alluréd with my pipes' delight,
Whose pleasing soundé shrilléd far about,
  Or thither led by chance, I know not right:
Whom, when I askéd from what place he came,
  And how he hight (was called), *himself he did yclepe*
      (style)
The Shepherd of the Oceän by name,
  And said he came far from the main sea deep.

Spenser went on to describe how Raleigh in his
turn started to make music:

His song was all a lamentable lay
Of great unkindness and of usage hard
Of Cynthia, the Lady of the Sea (Queen Elizabeth)
Which from her faultless presence him debarred.

That pastoral interlude came to an end, and Raleigh took Spenser back with him to London, where the first three books of 'Faerie Queene' were published in 1590. Raleigh was again in favour, and Essex, for the second time, in the shadows. The impetuous youth had married Sir Philip Sidney's widow, the daughter of Walsingham, the Secretary of State, without informing the Queen. Elizabeth, who liked her favourites to remain unmarried, was furious for a time, and before Essex was allowed back at Court he had to agree that his Countess should always live a retired life, in the country. Raleigh, in the meantime, was able to present Spenser to his Sovereign and to obtain for him an annual pension of fifty pounds: 'All this for a song' is said to have been the comment of Burghley, the Treasury watchdog. Among the poems appended to the first edition of 'Faerie Queene' was a fine commendatory sonnet by Raleigh, and an answering sonnet by Spenser to Raleigh, which opened:

To thee, that art the summer's nightingale,
Thy sovereign Goddess's most dear delight . . .

Raleigh's principal poetical work, which he was composing in Ireland, is lost, except for a long

fragment from the twenty-first and last book. It
was entitled 'The Ocean's love to Cynthia'
(Elizabeth), and Spenser implied that it embodied a
lament for the passing of the Queen's favour which
it made a bid to recapture. As such it happily
served its purpose. The writing of verse was a
normal, gentlemanly accomplishment in the Elizabethan age, and it was bad form in a man of fashion
to rate it highly. Most of Raleigh's poetry, therefore, is lost. What survives is distinguished, for the
most part, by taut, strung, melancholy rhythms,
but it is of high quality. It expressed the search-
ing, unsatisfied spirit of an age that had lost its
faith:

> *Go, soul, the body's guest,*
> *Upon a thankless errand!*
>
> *Say to the Court it glows*
> *And shines like rotten wood,*
> *Say to the Church it shows*
> *What's good, and does no good.*
> *If Church and State reply,*
> *Then give them both the lie!*
>
> *Tell faith it's fled the city,*
> *Tell how the country erreth,*
>
> . . . .

That note of disillusionment was sounded again in
the best of all his poems, 'The Pilgrimage':

Give me my scallop-shell of quiet,
  My staff of faith to walk upon,
My scrip of joy, immortal diet,
  My bottle of salvation,
My gown of glory, hope's true gage;
  And thus I'll make my pilgrimage.

Then, by that happy, blissful day
  More peaceful pilgrims shall I see
That have cast off their rags of clay
  And walk apparell'd fresh like me.
    I'll take them first
    To quench their thirst
  And taste of nectar suckets,
    At those clear wells
    Where sweetness dwells,
Drawn up by saints in crystal buckets.

Raleigh's sense of the vanity of earthly pleasures was expressed once more in the lines written in reply to his friend Christopher Marlowe's poem, 'The Passionate Shepherd to His Love.' Marlowe had written:

Come, live with me and by my love,
And we will all the pleasures prove
That hills and valleys, dales and fields,
Woods, or steepy mountains yield.

But Raleigh pictured the shepherdess declining in terms of extreme disillusionment:

If all the world, and love, were young,
And truth on every shepherd's tongue,
These pretty pleasures might me move
To live with thee, and be thy love.
Thy gowns, thy shoes, thy beds of roses,
Thy cap, thy kirtle, and thy posies,
Soon break, soon wither, soon forgotten—
In folly ripe, in reason rotten.

Raleigh's surviving poetry is scanty in amount and his reputation has been damaged as a result of the wrongful ascription to him of a number of worthless pieces. Some of the poems which are certainly his, express personal moods, but it would be dangerous to read too much into them. The wistful, plaintive note which informed so much of his verse, needs to be contrasted with the robust, and self-sufficient mood which characterized much of his prose ; and which induced him to declare unequivocally that the ' ordinary theme and argument of history is war.'

When Raleigh returned from Ireland with Edmund Spenser early in 1590, he renewed his efforts to obtain an active command at sea. He nearly succeeded in obtaining the post of Vice-Admiral to Lord Thomas Howard in the expedition which was despatched in 1591 to intercept a Spanish treasure fleet. Sir Richard Grenville, in the *Revenge*, took Raleigh's place at the last moment and perished after a heroic battle against impossible odds. Raleigh immortalized the story in his first published prose work—*The Last Fight of the Revenge at Sea.* It was published towards the end of that year (1591), and nearly three centuries later (in 1878) it provided Tennyson with the material for a famous rollicking ballad. An extract from Raleigh's narrative will illustrate the quality of his prose:

' All the powder of the *Revenge* to the last barrel was now spent, all her pikes broken, forty of her best men slain, and the most part of the rest hurt. In the beginning of the fight she had but one hundred free from sickness, and fourscore and ten sick, laid in hold upon the ballast. A small troop to man such a ship, and a weak garrison to resist so mighty an army. By those hundred, all was sustained, the volleys, boardings, and enterings of fifteen ships of war, besides those which beat her at large. On the contrary,[1] the Spanish were always supplied with soldiers brought from every squadron; all manner of arms and powder at will. Unto ours there remained no comfort at all, no hope, no supply either of ships, men, or weapons; the masts all beaten overboard, all her tackle cut asunder, her upper work altogether razed, and in effect evened she was with the water, but the very foundation or bottom of a ship, nothing being left overhead either for flight or defence. Sir Richard, finding himself in this distress, and unable any longer to make resistance, having endured in this fifteen hours' fight the assault of fifteen several armadoes, all by turns aboard him, and by estimation eight hundred

[1] i.e. on the other hand.

shot of great artillery, besides many assaults and entries; and that he himself and the ship must needs be possessed by the enemy who were now all cast in a ring round about him; the *Revenge* not being able to move one way or other, but as she was moved with the waves and billow of the sea: commanded the master Gunner, whom he knew to be a most resolute man, to split and sink the ship, that thereby nothing might remain of glory or victory to the Spaniards, seeing in so many hours' fight, and with so great a navy, they were not able to take her, having had fifteen hours' time, fifteen thousand men, and fifty and three sail of men-of-war to perform it withal: and persuaded the company, or as many as he could induce, to yield themselves unto God, and to the mercy of none else; but as they had, like valiant, resolute men, repulsed so many enemies, they should not now shorten the honour of their nation by prolonging their own lives for a few hours, or a few days.

' The master Gunner readily condescended, and divers others; but the Captain and the Master were of another opinion, and besought Sir Richard to have care of them: alleging that the Spaniard would be as ready to entertain a composition as they were willing to offer the same: and that there being divers sufficient and valiant men yet living, and whose wounds were not mortal, they might do their country and Prince acceptable service hereafter. And (that where Sir Richard had alleged that the Spaniards should never glory to have taken one ship of Her Majesty's seeing that they had so long and so notably defended themselves) they answered that the ship had six foot of water in hold, three shot under water, which were so weakly stopped as with the first working of the sea she must needs sink, and was besides so crushed and bruised as she could never be removed out of the place.

' And as the matter was thus in dispute, and Sir Richard refusing to hearken to any of those reasons, the Master of the *Revenge* (while the Captain won unto him the greater party) was conveyed aboard the General, *Don Alfonso Bassan*. Who finding none over hasty to enter the *Revenge* again, doubting lest Sir Richard Grenville would have blown them up and himself, and perceiving by the report of the Master of the *Revenge* his dangerous disposition: yielded that all their lives should be saved, the Company sent for England, and the better sort to pay such reasonable ransom as their estate would bear, and in the mean season to be free from galley or imprisonment. To this he so much the rather condescended as well, I have said, for fear of further loss or mischief to themselves, as also for the desire he had to recover Sir Richard Grenville; whom, for his notable valour he seemed greatly to honour and admire.'

Sir Richard Grenville died of his wounds two days later, after being treated ' with all humanity ': and it is possible that Raleigh may later have been tempted to envy his fate. In the following year,

1592, he forfeited the Queen's favour, and was committed, for the first time, to the Tower.

Raleigh had succeeded in obtaining a commission as Admiral in command of an expedition to sack Panama and to plunder another Spanish treasure fleet. Once more, however, at the last moment the Queen refused to let him go. He was merely allowed to start the expedition on its course, before handing over the command to Sir Martin Frobisher (May, 1592). Raleigh accompanied the expedition as far as Cape Finisterre, and then returned to London to find the Court in an uproar and his Sovereign in a furious rage.

The cause of Raleigh's sudden fall from favour became the source of the greatest comfort and happiness which he was to know in life. He had for some years been carrying on an intrigue with one of the Queen's Maids of Honour, Elizabeth Throckmorton, daughter of a well-known diplomat of the previous generation. Raleigh had not intended to marry the girl, but as soon as the affair was discovered he married in haste, a few days before he sailed, in the vain hope of diverting the worst of the Queen's anger. The result was to bring down on Raleigh's head a renewed torrent of the royal fury. He was arrested as soon as he returned to London after his voyage to Cape Finisterre, and the wedded couple spent what should have been a delayed honeymoon in separate cells in the Tower.

Both were released after a few weeks, but Raleigh was not forgiven for five years. Lady Raleigh was never forgiven at all. The Queen treated her as though she were dead, and she never held any communication with her again.

From the Tower, in August 1592, Raleigh wrote to Sir Robert Cecil (later Earl of Salisbury) in the romantic language of the Court. The Queen was on a royal progress, and Raleigh's letter was, of course, intended for her eye:

' My heart was never broken till this day, that I hear the Queen goes away so far off, whom I have followed so many years with so great love and desire, on so many journeys, and am now left behind her, in a dark prison, alone. While she was yet near at hand, that I might hear of her once in two or three days, my sorrows were the less, but even now my heart is cast into the depth of all misery. I, that was wont to behold her riding like Alexander, walking like Venus, the gentle wind blowing her fair hair about her pure cheeks like a nymph [the Queen, in fact, was then a woman of sixty, but she relished such flattery], sometimes sitting in the shade like a Goddess, sometimes singing like an angel, sometimes playing like Orpheus. Behold the sorrow of this world. Once amiss hath bereaved me of all! '

Cecil must have smiled when he received that letter. Elizabeth's Court, high-spirited as it was, was no more prepared to condone laxity than was Queen Victoria's. In Elizabeth's eyes the Maids of Honour were as sacred as Vestal Virgins; and she always treated her favourites as though they were her personal property. It was impossible for any of them to marry without provoking an emotional storm. Raleigh's slip delighted his enemies, but the Queen's affection proved to be deep enough to preserve him from ruin, and in his marriage he was wonderfully fortunate. Lady Raleigh was loving, gentle, loyal, self-effacing, and supremely courageous through all the misfortunes which later overtook them. They both loved Sherborne, where it is possible to think that Raleigh's spirit still lingers. It was at Sherborne that their first child, another Walter, was born in 1594.

Raleigh fretted at his imprisonment for what he termed in another letter to Cecil ' one frail misfortune.' He wrote to Lord Howard of Effingham about ' this unfortunate accident.' The immediate occasion of his release was the happy outcome of the expedition which he had organized and started in the early part of 1592. It captured off the Azores the *Madre de Dios* (Mother of God) and she proved to be the richest prize ever taken.

The *Madre de Dios* was a seven-decker laden with a fabulous treasure. Her cargo consisted of masses of diamonds, rubies, and pearls, a great quantity of gold and silver, silks, perfumes, spices, and other valuable commodities. When she was brought into Dartmouth the West Country went temporarily mad, and an orgy of looting took place which the authorities were for a time unable to restrain. Sir Robert Cecil was ordered immediately to post to

Dartmouth in order to restore order, and he insisted on taking Raleigh with him.

Raleigh's name commanded fear and respect in the West Country, and Cecil was astonished by the warmth of Raleigh's reception. Treasure to the value of at least one hundred and forty-one thousand pounds in the money of that age was recovered. Raleigh's services earned the release of himself and of his wife from imprisonment, but he complained bitterly of the paltry share of the prize money which he received. He had organized the expedition on a joint-stock basis, in partnership with the Queen, the Earl of Cumberland, and a syndicate of London merchants. The Admirals in command, Sir Martin Frobisher and Sir John Borough, although tactically, of course, independent, had acted in accordance with his strategic dispositions.

Elizabeth took the lion's share, and Raleigh had to be content with the retention of all the offices which he had been in danger of losing. He was not, however, allowed to return to Court, so that his office of Captain of the Guard had to be performed by deputy. Nevertheless, he still possessed his palace in the Strand, and all his other properties, and as he had time on his hands, he took to attending the House of Commons, where he pleaded for religious liberty. Five years were to pass before the full sunshine of his Sovereign's favour was restored, and the sun was then seen to be setting rapidly. The shock which Raleigh had suffered was painful and severe, and it braced him to take himself in

hand. Thenceforward he was no longer entangled in Elizabeth's silken apron strings; he was faced squarely with the task of seeking new foundations to support the splendid superstructure which he had raised; and unfortunately he failed to find them.

* 3 *

Into the Storm

WHILE RALEIGH, after his eclipse, was fighting hard to re-establish his position and to recover the Queen's favour, his enemies, naturally, did their utmost to injure him and keep him down. They blocked his colonizing work in Ireland, and prevented him from obtaining licences for the export of timber; they interfered with his jurisdictions in Devon and Cornwall; they hoped for a time to ruin him by instigating a formal charge of atheism against him.

Raleigh's religious opinions were a subject of controversy throughout his life; and that was partly, but not entirely, due to the magnetism of his personality. He was incautious in speech and action, and his restless, daring spirit caused him at one period of his life to call in question all conventional beliefs. Durham House, Raleigh's London home in the Strand, and Sherborne Abbey, his principal country seat, were two centres of a brilliant society which included, among others, the Earls of Northumberland and Derby; Edmund Spenser and George Chapman, the poets; Christopher Marlowe.

the playwright; Thomas Hariot, the scientist; and a number of lesser men. Northumberland and Derby were considered to be eccentric noblemen on account of their interest in scientific experiments and in alchemy. The popular name for that circle was ' The School of Night '; its proceedings were harmless enough but they evoked wild rumours at times which gave rise to a certain amount of baseless scandal. William Shakespeare who was attached to a rival set centred around Essex House, poked fun, in *Love's Labour's Lost*, one of his youthful works, at the proceedings of the ' School of Night '.

The storm broke over Raleigh's head early in 1594, shortly after his friend, Marlowe had been killed in a tavern brawl. Marlowe's reputation had been none too savoury, and if he had lived he would have been arrested on a charge of blasphemy and atheism. Raleigh was most unjustly suspected, in some quarters, of having had a hand in Marlowe's death in order to avert any dangerous revelations. A Commission of Inquiry was subsequently set up to investigate the attitude of Raleigh and others to conventional religious beliefs; it began its hearings at Cerne Abbas, Dorsetshire, near Sherborne, on 21st March, 1594. Raleigh was accused of having conducted a school of atheism, and there was widespread popular excitement.

Raleigh's enemies found that they had badly overreached themselves. Their case, which depended upon hearsay, fell to pieces; but it was widely known that Raleigh and some of his closest friends had ceased to be orthodox Christians. Eager to reconcile belief in God with exciting scientific speculations, Raleigh was attracted towards deism; and his enemies seized that chance to discredit him if they could.

Experience of the instability of human greatness caused Raleigh to yearn for the support of strong religious faith. But he was not much more successful in arriving at any satisfying philosophy than he was in devizing a settled plan on which to organize his life. He was detached from the Catholic tradition in either its Catholic or Anglican forms; and he was equally detached from the new Puritan mood which had already captured men like Walsingham and which, after a severe but temporary setback during the 1590s, was destined to sweep the country during the first part of the next century. In those circumstances Raleigh pleaded for tolerance and did his best to promote a spirit of free inquiry. He opposed an Act to make attendance at Church compulsory. He pondered deeply and often on the mysteries of religion, but he could never wholly suppress an element of materialism:

' To what end ', he wrote, ' were religion if there were no reward? And what reward is there if the souls do not live for ever? '

He advised his son to please God lest he be punished, and to marry not for love but for position; he was perhaps always a little too much inclined to confuse the soul's adventure with a privateering expedition. But if his outlook was a trifle crude in some respects, there was nothing hypocritical about it, and few of his contemporaries had a right to cast stones.

As it was, the scandal of atheism pursued Raleigh to the grave. Some time after his execution in 1618, the Archbishop of Canterbury, George Abbot, wrote unkindly to his friend, Sir Thomas Roe, a famous ambassador and traveller, that Raleigh had formerly:

'questioned God's being and omnipotence, which that just Judge made good upon himself in overtumbling his estate, but last of all in bringing him to an execution by law, when he died a religious and Christian death.'

When the attack on him collapsed, Raleigh's mind reverted at once to the privateering business which had paid such splendid dividends two years previously in the affair of the *Madre de Dios*. He wrote to Lord Howard of Effingham on 21st June, 1594, begging him to approach the Queen on his behalf, and saying that he would be content to serve under the Admiral 'in the place of a poor mariner or soldier'. He cannot have intended to be taken literally; but his thoughts were already centred on an expedition to 'Guiana', the modern Venezuela. He was aware that he had grown somewhat soft during the 1580s. He was always subject to sea-sickness; he loved luxury and fine clothes; he had come to acquiesce too easily in the Queen's reluctance to allow him to go to sea. It used to be said of him that, despite his passion for the sea, whenever he had occasion to visit the south bank of the Thames from his palace in the Strand, he would always go round by London Bridge in preference to being ferried across the river. Thenceforward he was to make amends.

One of Raleigh's most attractive qualities is that he seemed to retain the heart of a schoolboy until the end of his life. It was not simply that he loved adventure and that his mind was always open to whatever was marvellous and exciting; he was invariably ready to translate his enthusiasm into action and to stake his all upon whatever interest had taken possession of his mind. During the early 1590s he became convinced that somewhere in the undiscovered country between the headwaters of the Amazon and Orinoco rivers lay the land of El Dorado. He thought that that land was ruled by a potentate called the Emperor of Guiana, who owned an infinite treasure of gold, silver, and precious stones, and who had received, in addition, a part of the treasure of the Incas from the fallen Empire of Peru: 'There was nothing', Raleigh wrote, 'in his country whereof he had not the counterfeit in gold.' The fable of El Dorado, which was firmly credited in Spain, had passed into contemporary mythology, and by the end of the sixteenth century there was a considerable literature on the subject. The story had become inextricably confused with timeless myths and legends. But Raleigh, who read and spoke Spanish as well as French, after interviewing numerous travellers, studying such maps as were available, poring over books, and brooding greatly over the subject in his gardens at Sherborne and his turret study at Durham Palace, was certain that the land of El Dorado was no fable, but a concrete reality. He exposed some of the grounds of his belief in his book, *The Discovery of the Large, Rich, and Beautiful Empire of Guiana* (1596). He wrote there of:

' people whose heads appear not above their shoulders, which, though it may be thought a mere fable, yet for mine own part I am resolved it is true because every child in the provinces of Arromaia and Canuri affirms the same.'

After Shakespeare had read that, he made Othello, when he was wooing Desdemona, speak of:

> *The Anthropophagi, and men whose heads*
> *Do grow beneath their shoulders.*

The amazing and almost fabulous wealth which Spain was at that time drawing every year from the mines of South and Central America helped to predispose Raleigh's contemporaries to believe that other territories in the New World might provide explorers and conquerors from Europe with similar or even greater rewards. In 1594, accordingly, Raleigh sent out one of his trusted lieutenants, Jacob Whiddon, to reconnoitre the Orinoco river. Whiddon's report was inconclusive, but he brought back numerous travellers' tales, most of which Raleigh knew already by heart, of the country's boundless wealth of gold and precious stones. It is quite possible that the Jesuit missionaries encouraged those reports in the hope of inducing such men as Raleigh to co-operate involuntarily with them in opening up a country where they had a duty to spread the Gospel.

Raleigh was certain that he now held the clues which would lead him to fabulous wealth, such as Pizarro had found when he overturned the Inca Empire in Peru. He dreamed of conquering the Empire of Guiana for the Queen and of governing it himself; he bombarded the members of the Privy Council, particularly Robert Cecil, with letters; and he finally received authority from the Queen to lead an expedition up the Orinoco into the land of his dreams. It is significant that the patent was addressed to ' our servant, Sir Walter Raleigh '; and that the customary words ' trusty and well-beloved ' were omitted.

The expedition, consisting of five ships, sailed on 6th February, 1595. It was commanded by Raleigh, who reached the New World for the first time when he landed at Curapan, Trinidad, on 22nd March, 1595. Three of the five ships had turned back on the way. Raleigh's first action was to burn a Spanish settlement and to seize the island's governor, Antonio de Berrio, whom he treated with great ceremony and used as a source of information. He pursued, from the first, a policy of conciliating the natives whom he hoped, later, to rule. The Spaniards had done themselves great harm by practising savage cruelties towards them. Raleigh called a meeting

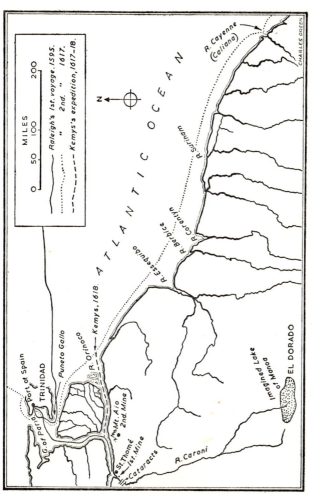

RALEIGH'S VOYAGES TO GUIANA

of the native chiefs, showed them a portrait of the Queen, and said that she was resolved to free all peoples who were oppressed by Spain. That policy was highly successful.

Raleigh's prisoner knew that a new Spanish expedition was already on its way from Seville to discover El Dorado. He tried, therefore, to dissuade his captor from undertaking his voyage to the mainland. That was, of course, futile. Raleigh knew already, from captured documents, about the Spanish expedition which was under way, and he believed that the quest for El Dorado had become a race for time with Spain, in which he held a winning lead.

He crossed the dividing strait to the mainland, and explored the Orinoco in an old galley, with a barge, two wherries, and an ordinary ship's boat in attendance. His party consisted of 100 men with provisions for one month, and it suffered great hardships. Of his own galley he wrote:

' I will undertake there was never any prison in England more unsavoury and loathsome, especially to myself, who had, for many years before, been dieted and cared for in a sort far differing.'

After fifteen nightmarish days they fell in with a party of friendly natives and reached some country which seemed attractive. They tasted pineapple— the royal fruit which James I later declared was too delicious for a subject; they fed on the flesh of armadilloes. They rowed 400 miles up-river from the sea, and in the heart of the Indian country

Raleigh won the loyalty and affection of the natives. He arranged alliances and promised to return; the memory of his journey remained as a legend for many generations. But the rains were coming on; the river was rising; no gold mines—no fabulous empire—had been discovered. With heavy hearts the explorers returned to the coast, still convinced that they were on the right trail, and that they had been on the verge of success. They comforted themselves with the thought that, as a result of their efforts, the English flag would presently be waving over as wide an empire as that covered by Spain's.

The journey home was very arduous. Raleigh was prevented by storms from visiting Virginia, as he had intended, to seek his lost colonists. He reached England at the end of August, 1595, after burning three Spanish settlements on the way.

In the account of his voyage which he published in the following year, Raleigh described Guiana as the 'magazine of all rich metals'. Peru and Mexico had been sacked, and their wealth had turned the King of Spain 'in a few years from a poor King of Castile to the greatest monarch of this part of the world'. He urged his countrymen to be swift and resolute to possess themselves of Guiana, a country 'that hath yet her maidenhead, never sacked, turned, nor wrought; . . . the graves have not been opened for gold, the mines not broken with sledges; nor their images pulled down out of their temples '.

But the Court smiled because he had failed to bring back any gold, and opinion remained chilly and apathetic. Many were privately delighted that Raleigh had been made to look foolish. The Queen was ageing and was clearly not immortal, whatever poets and flatterers might write or say. Her principal ministers and courtiers were busy intriguing and forming alliances among themselves with a view to securing their places and fortunes whenever a change of sovereign should occur. It suited them well that Raleigh's attention should be diverted from Whitehall to El Dorado.

There was, moreover, one other factor to be remembered. The generation of inspired pirates, with which Raleigh was associated by family ties and personal inclination, was passing away. Gilbert was drowned in 1583; Grenville was killed in 1591; Frobisher was killed in 1594; Hawkins died at sea in 1595; and Drake died also at sea in 1596. The trade lacked fresh recruits of the calibre of those who had passed on, and Raleigh, whom the Spaniards feared and called ' Guateral ' was becoming dangerously isolated.

As he was still prevented from resuming his old position at Court, Raleigh fretted at Sherborne, or at Bath, where he sometimes took the waters. He sent a third expedition to Guiana on 1st January, 1596, which was commanded by his faithful friend, Laurence Keymis, a former Fellow of Balliol. Keymis had served as Raleigh's second-in-command during the previous year. A fourth expedition was

despatched to Guiana later in the year 1596, and
although the results were negative, Raleigh continued to do everything in his power to stimulate
public interest in Guiana.

He wrote on 13th November, 1595, to Sir Robert
Cecil:

' I humbly beseech you to move her Majesty that
none be suffered to soil the enterprize, and that
those kings of the borders which are, by my labour,
peril, and charge, won to her Majesty's love and
obedience, be not, by other pilferers, lost again.
I hope I shall be thought worthy to direct those
actions I have, at mine own charges, laboured in;
and to govern that country which I have discovered,
and hope to conquer for the Queen, without her
cost. I am sending away a barque to the country
to comfort and assure the people that they despair
not, nor yield to any composition with other
nations . . .

' If I be thought unworthy to be employed, or
that, because of my disgrace, all men fear to adventure with me—if it may not be otherwise—I wish
some other, of better sufficiency, might undertake it,
that the Queen lose not that which she shall never
find again . . .'

Raleigh went on to refer to precious stones he had
found, but he did not sound very convincing:

' I have sent you one which was cut here, which
I think is amethyst, and hath the strong blush of
carnation. But I assure myself that there are not
more diamonds to be found in the East Indies than

are to be found in Guiana; which you see also
verified by the relation of the Spanish letters.

' I have another, cut, of another sort; and if it
it be no diamond, yet it is exceeding any diamond
in beauty. But I am not in haste to let it go out of
my fingers. But these stones bear witness of better,
and there is enough for all the world if we have the
grace (patience). But we must cast so many
doubts, and this dolt and that gull must be satisfied,
or else all is nothing. If the Spaniard had been so
blockish and slothful, we had not feared now their
power, who, by their gold from thence, vex and
endanger all the estates of kings . . .'

Cecil, and his father, Burghley, were moved to
contribute something to Raleigh's follow-up expeditions in 1596, but the results were as inconclusive as
before. The devoted Keymis was certain that he
had been within an ace of discovering a valuable
gold mine, but few, save Raleigh, believed it. It
seemed that Raleigh, in his attempt to rebuild his
career on some foundation more substantial than
the Queen's favour, had been pursuing a will-o'-the-
wisp. The wise world smiled and remained in-
different, but Raleigh's book made a stir among
poets and children. It was often reprinted and
translated. Echoes from it occur in Shakespeare's
Othello and *The Tempest,* and in Milton's *Paradise
Lost.* Lesser poets, like Chapman, celebrated:

Guiana, whose rich seat are mines of gold.

He pictured the welcome which would await those who went there:

> *A world of savages fall tame before them,*
> *Storing their theft-free treasuries with gold.*

Such inspired poetical prospectuses made little appeal to Court or City. The Queen was old; the Court was bored by Guiana. There was no prospect of success in that age for any scheme of colonizing the country, although Raleigh dreamed much more of empire than of gold. He knew that he could only succeed if he were able to bring home strong, irrefutable proofs of easy wealth to be gained. He failed to do that and the project ended in total failure. But he was not, in all respects, pursuing a mirage. Long after he was dead, gold and diamonds were mined in Venezuela; and both are important industries in that country to-day. The greatest wealth, however, was to arise from a mineral whose use would have fascinated his eager, inquiring, open mind. More than two centuries after his death petroleum made Venezuela one of the world's richest areas.

Raleigh's account of his great-hearted enterprise can still be read with pleasure. All his life he was as vital and enthusiastic as a boy, and it is that spirit which has helped to enshrine his fame.

II

In the year 1596 the nation braced itself to strike a supreme blow at the Spanish enemy who had recently renewed his menace of invasion. The strongest raiding expedition of the reign was organized to sail to Cadiz—Spain's chief port—and to do as much damage as it could to the enemy's naval power. It was a combined operation with Lords Howard of Effingham and Essex in joint supreme command of the sea and land armaments. Lord Thomas Howard served as Vice-Admiral; Raleigh as Rear-Admiral; and Sir Francis Vere as Commander of the Land Forces. When the entire force was assembled at Plymouth, it consisted of seventeen ships of the Royal Navy, and seventy-six hired ships, mustered in four squadrons of approximately equal strength. Those ships carried some 6,500 sailors and an equal number of soldiers. Included with those were about 1,000 gentlemen volunteers. In addition, there was a squadron of twenty-four Dutch vessels carrying 2,600 men. The English squadrons were led by Howard of Effingham, flying his flag in the *Ark Royal*; by Essex in the *Repulse*; Thomas Howard in the *Merhonour*; and Raleigh in the *Warspite*.

The difficulty of collecting men to serve in that great operation was illustrated in a letter from Raleigh to Robert Cecil, dated 4th May, 1596. Raleigh said that he had been in the neighbourhood of Gravesend ' hunting after runaway mariners, and dragging in the mire from ale-house to ale-house'. Essex made an example of two deserters, whom he hanged on Plymouth Hoe. There was delay and confusion before starting, and petty disputes took place between the commanders. It was said, when everything was settled at last, that the officers' display of gold and silver lace on shipboard was the most dazzling that had ever been seen.

The fleet sailed on 3rd June, 1596, and came to anchor a fortnight later off Cadiz. After the battle which followed, many Spaniards who had watched it from the doomed city, said that they had never seen a sight more beautiful or more terrible. The enemy was taken completely by surprise. The Duke of Medina Sidonia, who had led the Armada to its doom, was serving as Governor of Andalusia. He hastened to Cadiz with various Spanish commanders, who had been on leave; they left their pleasant houses in Seville, and the surrounding orange-groves, while a line of powerful galleons put out of the harbour and took up position to guard the town. Raleigh had been ordered to cruise with his squadron along the coast and to prevent any enemy ships escaping from, or entering, the harbour. In his absence a council of war, held on the *Ark Royal*, decided to land the troops and to assault the city immediately, before joining action with the enemy's fleet.

When Raleigh, on the morning of 20th June, returned from his cruise along the coast, the troops had already started to disembark in a choppy sea

under the walls of fort of San Sebastian. He saw
boats capsize in the rough water, and he appreciated
at once that a wrong decision had been taken. He
considered that the enemy's fleet should first have
been brought to action and destroyed. He considered, further, that the landing operation which
had been begun at that point and at that moment
was unlikely to succeed.

He had himself rowed at once to Essex in the
Repulse, and begged him to stop the landing before
it was too late. In Raleigh's words:

' The Earl excused himself, and laid it to the
Lord Admiral, who, he said, would not consent to
enter with the fleet till the town was first possessed.
All the commanders and gentlemen present besought me to dissuade the attempt, for they all
perceived the danger, and were resolved that the
most part could not but perish in the sea, ere they
came to set foot on ground, and if any arrived on
shore, yet were they sure to have their boats cast on
their heads; and that twenty men in so desperate
a descent would have defeated them all. The Earl
prayed me to persuade the Lord Admiral.'

Raleigh hastened to Howard's flagship, the *Ark
Royal*, and secured from him an order counter-
manding the landing. He returned to Essex armed
with that and with a new order to prepare immediately to bring the enemy's fleet, which had so far
remained passive, to action. From his pinnace he
shouted to Essex, who was leaning with others over
the rail, ' Entramos ', meaning that the landing was

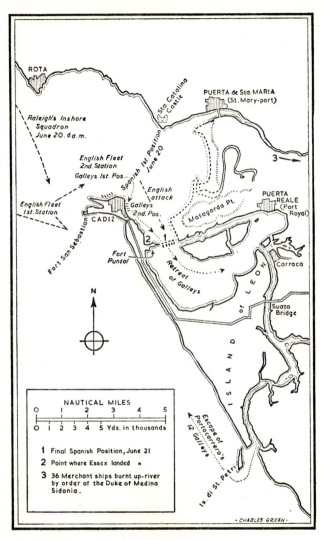

ROTA

Raleigh's Inshore
Squadron
June 20. 6 a.m.

English Fleet
2nd. Station
Galleys 1st. Pos.

English Fleet
1st. Station

Fort San Sebastian

CADIZ

Sta. Catalina
Castle

Spanish 1st. Position
June 20

English
attack

Galleys
2nd. Pos.

Fort
Puntal

PUERTA de Sta. MARIA
(St. Mary-port)

3 →

Matagorda Pt.

Retreat
of Galleys

PUERTA
REALE
(Port
Royal)

Carraca

ISLAND of LEON

Suazo
Bridge

N

NAUTICAL MILES
0   1   2   3   4   5
0 1 2 3 4 5 Yds. in thousands

1 Final Spanish Position, June 21
2 Point where Essex landed
3 36 Merchant ships burnt up-river
   by order of the Duke of Medina
   Sidonia.

Escape of
Portocarero's
12 Galleys

Is. di St. Petri.

· CHARLES GREEN ·

CADIZ HARBOUR

cancelled and that the fleet would sail into the harbour. Essex cheered, and flung his cap into the sea.

It was late by the time all the troops and boats had been received back on board the ships. That night a council of war was held, and the order of battle decided for the following day. The honour of leading the van was accorded to Raleigh, and at daybreak he led his squadron into the narrow channel which protected the entrance to the harbour: some of the seven galleys, sheltering under the walls of the town, together with the batteries on shore, fired on his ships, but Raleigh ignored them. He answered with a scornful flourish of trumpets, and pushed on to where the four great galleons, the *St. Philip*, the *St. Mathew*, the *St. Thomas*, and the *St. Andrew*, were drawn up in line ahead at the narrowest point of the channel. As soon as Raleigh closed, a general fleet action began. During an early stage of that engagement, the galleys Raleigh had scorned crept past him, hugging the shore, to join the main Spanish fleet. Raleigh said that he ' bestowed a benediction amongst them ' as they passed. The first stage of the action lasted about three hours, while Raleigh impatiently awaited the arrival of flyboats, which were wanted to assist the boarding operation. During all that time the enemy enjoyed the advantage of superior fire-power, for they were able to bring their broadside guns to bear, whereas the English, despite their superior numbers, were in line abreast, and could only use their bow pieces. While that deadlock lasted the English commanders were manœuvring so hard to steal from Raleigh the honour of the van position that the channel became blocked and the flyboats were delayed: 'But always', Raleigh wrote, 'I must, without glory, say for myself, that I held single, in the head of all'. Raleigh finally paid Essex a brief visit, and informed him that he proposed to hazard his ships by boarding the enemy without the aid of flyboats. The excitement of battle had drawn the two men close together; Essex readily agreed, and promised to second Raleigh's attempt in person.

Raleigh now altered the disposition of a part of his squadron from line abreast to line ahead. He laid his own vessel, the *Warspite*, alongside the great *St. Philip*, one of those against which Grenville had fought his last fight in the *Revenge*, seven years before. He was resolved, he wrote, to be 'revenged for the *Revenge*, or to second her with mine own life'. Boarders were already being piped over the side when, suddenly, the enemy's resistance collapsed. The great galleons were burnt or driven ashore, and Raleigh described the situation which developed:

'The spectacle was very lamentable on their side; for many drowned themselves; many, half-burnt, leaped into the water; very many, hanging by the ropes' ends by the ships' sides, under the water even to the lips; many swimming with grievous wounds, stricken under water and put out of their pain;

S.W.R.   F

and withal so huge a fire and such tearing of the
ordnance of the great *Philip* and the rest, when the
fire came to them, as, if any man had desire to see
hell itself, it was there most lively figured. Our-
selves spared the lives of all after the victory; but
the Flemings, who did little or nothing in the
fight, used merciless slaughter, till they were by
myself and, afterwards, by my Lord Admiral
beaten off.'

In the moment of victory Raleigh sustained a
painful leg wound which prevented him from
taking part in the storming of the town. He was
left with a slight limp for the rest of his life. As
soon as it was clear that the fleet action had resulted
in total victory, Essex gave the order for the troops
to disembark. The enemy offered some resistance,
but it was swept aside, and Vere quickly stormed
the town ' with a sudden fury '. Raleigh had himself carried ashore to see what was happening, and
even tried to mount a horse. But he was in great
pain, and had to be carried back to the *Warspite* and
laid in his berth.

The fleet was almost deserted. Officers and men
had all rushed ashore to join in the sack of Cadiz.
In the meantime, a great treasure fleet, which had
been sheltering in the roadstead of the harbour,
slipped its anchors and escaped up-river. Raleigh
had urged that it should be attacked immediately,
but the ships were almost deserted and nothing
could be done. Negotiations were opened with the
merchants of Seville and Cadiz for the treasure

fleet's ransom; but Medina Sidonia, with a great nobleman's proper contempt for merchants' interests, put a stop to them on 23rd June by ordering the ships to be burnt with their contents. By so doing he successfully prevented any additional advantage from accruing to his country's enemies.

Cadiz was sacked, but the victors used moderation. Violence to civilians was forbidden under pain of death, and Philip II paid tribute to the conduct of the English. Some atrocities were, however, committed by their Dutch allies. Much booty was collected, and a vast sum was promised as ransom for many of the leading citizens of the place, who were taken as hostages to England.

Cadiz was evacuated on 4th July, when the fleet sailed for home. Essex had urged that it should be retained as a permanent base as, later, Gibraltar was seized and retained. But the cost, and the difficulty of maintaining it, would have made that impossible. Commanders-in-Chief at that period had delegated to them the power of conferring knighthoods. After the battle no less than 66 knights were made, which caused laughter in England and helped to cheapen that honour for many years. Five knights only had been made after the victory over the Armada. The fleet, on its way home, raided Faro, where the fine library of Bishop Osorius was carried off. It later became the nucleus of the Bodleian Library at Oxford.

With his material reward for the great victory, Raleigh remained extremely dissatisfied:

' Many rich prisoners were given to the land commanders ... some had prisoners for sixteen thousand ducats; some for twenty thousand; some for ten thousand; and, besides, great houses of merchandize. What the Generals have gotten, I know least; they protest it is little. For my own part I have gotten a lame leg and deformed. For the rest, either I spake too late, or it was otherwise resolved. I have not wanted good words, and exceeding kind and regardful usage. But I have possession of naught but poverty and pain.'

Raleigh did, in fact, reap some material reward, but his greatest triumph lay in the goodwill he had earned in the fleet and among the soldiers. He shared, with Essex, the honours of the victory, and his fellow-commanders were generous in their praise. He had always been popular in Cornwall and in Devon, but he was disappointed to find, on his return, that he was still heartily disliked in the country as a whole, and that the Queen, although kinder, remained distant. Essex, however, who was the popular favourite as well as the Queen's, for a time laid aside his former enmity. A typical comment came from Anthony Standen, a staunch follower of Essex. Standen accompanied his hero to Cadiz, and on 5th July, he wrote to Burghley:

' Sir Walter Raleigh did, in my judgment, no man better, and his artillery most effect. I never knew the gentleman until this time, and am sorry for it, for there are in him excellent things besides his valour; and the observation he hath in this voyage used with my Lord of Essex hath made me love him.'

Not unnaturally Raleigh hoped that his services at Cadiz would effect his full reinstatement at Court and establish him at last on a firm foundation in the popular regard. That was not to be, but he derived an apparent advantage from drawing close to Sir Robert Cecil, who had just been appointed Secretary of State, as well as to Essex. Those two contrasting figures, Cecil and Essex, were now, with the exception of Cecil's father, the aged Burghley, the most powerful men in the land. Cecil, later first Earl of Salisbury, was a hunchback, but a born administrator and a great worker; he was subtle, cold, and reserved. He never sought the limelight, but his penetrating intelligence was always at the centre of affairs. Essex, physically superb, incapable of concealment, wayward, courageous, magnificent, had the world at his feet. He was the spoilt darling of the Court and Nation, and was still aged only thirty. To the country at large it was he, not Raleigh, who was the hero of Cadiz. Edmund Spenser hailed him:

Great England's glory and the world's wide wonder,
Whose dreadful name late through all Spain did thunder.
Fair branch of Honour, flower of Chivalry,
That fillest England with thy triumph's fame,
Joy have thou of thy famous victory!

The impression made by Essex on his countrymen at that time cannot easily be exaggerated. Shakespeare himself was moved to introduce into his prologue to the fifth act of the play, *King Henry the Fifth*, which was first performed three years later while Essex was suppressing a rebellion in Ireland, a contemporary allusion which must have raised, and been intended to raise, a loud cheer from the groundlings:

> *Were now the General of our gracious Empress—*
> *As in good time he may—from Ireland coming,*
> *Bringing rebellion broachéd on his sword,*
> *How many would the peaceful city quit*
> *To welcome him!*

Even Philip II, after Cadiz, said that it was extraordinary to find such a perfect nobleman among a nation of heretics.

Although still excluded from Court, Raleigh worked hard during the winter of 1596-7 on the task of bringing Robert Cecil and Essex together. They dined constantly at each other's houses and became very intimate. To the world it appeared that a triumvirate was being formed to take control of the situation as the Queen's glorious reign moved stormily towards its end. Raleigh believed that he was entering upon the most successful period of his life, and it suited Cecil to humour him.

Cecil was convinced that he could not work permanently with either Essex or Raleigh, unless he were to abandon the political system instituted by his father, Lord Burghley. He was resolved to continue that system, and to put a stop at the first opportunity to the long war with Spain. He played, accordingly, with both men in a manner which must be termed treacherous, while taking advantage of Essex's hot-headedness and of Raleigh's trustful and complacent blindness. Regarding himself as responsible for his country's safety and prosperity, Cecil considered that his methods were justified; and the rebellion and execution of Essex was followed less suddenly and only a little less dramatically by the ruin and destruction of Raleigh.

* 4 *

The Silver Cord is Loosed

RALEIGH'S RETURN to Court was delayed for nearly a year after the return of the victorious fleet from Cadiz. Much of that time, inevitably, was devoted to intrigue with his new political allies. On 24th January, 1597, he wrote Cecil a very human letter of sympathy on Lady Cecil's death:

' Sorrows ', he said, ' are dangerous companions, converting bad into evil, and evil into worse . . . The mind that entertaineth them is as the earth and dust whereon sorrows and adversities of the world do, as the beasts of the field, tread, trample, and defile . . . Sorrows draw not the dead to life, but the living to death . . .

' Yours, beyond the power of words to utter.'

Raleigh seldom permitted sorrows or adversities to prey upon his mind. After the death of Cecil's wife the Raleighs were kind to Cecil's son, Will, who was a delicate boy. They had him to stay for long periods at Sherborne, and watched carefully over his health and his studies. It was to that child, after he had succeeded his father as Lord

Salisbury, that Raleigh later dedicated his *History of the World.*

In May, 1597, Raleigh was greatly cheered by being allowed to return to Court. The next month he resumed his old office of Captain of the Guard, and was used once more as graciously by the Queen as he had ever been. But the aged woman's pulses no longer thrilled when he rode beside her, or came into her room, and the former convention of courtly adoration was never resumed between them. The Queen was nearing her end; all men were beginning to seem remote and ineffectual shadows to her. Only in the case of Essex were the old conventions retained. She followed eagerly his every movement.

Raleigh was given a contract to provision the fleet for a new expedition against Spain, and none knew better how to turn such an assignment to profit. It was generally believed that he would soon realize a long-cherished ambition to enter the Privy Council. He was so accustomed to being called into consultation by the Council that there were moments when he almost forgot to feel his exclusion from it as a grievance. For some months Raleigh had every reason to be satisfied with the fruits of his new political alignment. He was once again a factor of the first importance in the State, although his foundations remained precarious.

The new expedition against Spain was prepared on an ambitious scale. The English at war are like terriers; once they have gripped an enemy by the

throat they are incapable of letting him go. In the
autumn of 1596 it was known that Philip II had
collected an armada at Ferrol, in North Spain,
which was believed to be aimed at Ireland. That
fleet put to sea, whether as an exercise or in earnest
it was hard to decide, but it ran into foul weather
and returned quickly to port. Feverish preparations
were being made to furnish it with everything need-
ful, and despatches flowed from Philip's headquarters in the Escurial, to Ferrol, in an endless
stream. The enemy, it was evident, was still
dangerous, and in England the decision was taken
to strike a fresh blow at him. It was hoped that it
would be as successful as the previous year's, and
that the tactics used at Cadiz would be repeated
successfully at Ferrol. The plan was to attack the
Spanish fleet in the port of Ferrol, and afterwards
to sail to the Azores and to intercept a convoy of
treasure ships known to be due from the West
Indies. Three squadrons of English with one
squadron of Dutch ships were assembled at Plymouth for the operation. Essex served as Commander-in-Chief of the combined sea and land
forces, and as commander of one of the three squadrons. Lord Thomas Howard, as Vice-Admiral,
commanded the second squadron, and Raleigh, as
Rear-Admiral, commanded the third. The fleet
sailed from Plymouth on 10th July, 1597, with
Raleigh flying his flag in the *Warspite* as before. In
his squadron were two great galleons, the *St. Andrew*
and the *St. Mathew*, which he had brought home as

prizes from Cadiz. There was a brilliant muster of gentlemen volunteers, including the Earls of Rutland and Southampton, and Lords Audley, Cromwell, Grey of Wilton, Rich, and Windsor. All hoped for glory and loot, but no laurels were to be reaped on that occasion by the arms either of England or of Spain.

The expedition was unfortunate from the outset. It ran immediately into such a violent storm that most of the ships, including the whole of Raleigh's squadron, were driven back to Plymouth or Falmouth. Only Thomas Howard, a tried and weather-beaten professional sailor, rode out the storm and led his squadron through it to the Spanish coast. He, too, returned, however, when he could find no suitable enemy to fight.

The fleet refitted and put to sea again on 17th August. But fresh storms were encountered and the squadrons lost touch with one another. Raleigh's mainyard snapped, and he was unable to tack about in an easterly wind so as to reach the agreed rendezvous off Finisterre on time. Essex, on his flagship, sprung a leak, and was late at the rendezvous. In his absence, most of Howard's squadron, with the Dutch squadron, followed Raleigh's lead to the second rendezvous off Lisbon. Essex in consequence had no fleet left with which to attack Ferrol and he, too, therefore, sailed to the rendezvous off Lisbon.

There were some high words between Essex and Raleigh over that mismanagement, but they soon reached an accord. Raleigh had received intelligence, which later proved to be false, that the enemy's fleet had sailed from Ferrol to the Azores in order to escort the treasure ships to Spain. It was resolved, accordingly, to sail immediately to the Azores with the object of destroying that fleet and capturing the treasure ships.

Essex's handling of the expedition seemed at that point to collapse. He hesitated, and issued no clear orders to his subordinate commanders; some thought that Terceira, the principal island in the Azores, should be attacked; others considered that it was too strongly defended. No final decision was taken at that time.

When the fleet assembled off Flores, Essex and Raleigh had a friendly meeting, and Raleigh, with his principal officers, dined on the Commander-in-Chief's flagship. They discussed, with great cordiality, the series of chances which had caused the abandonment of the proposed attack on Ferrol. While Raleigh was taking on board fresh water and provisions, Essex, with the remainder of the fleet, suddenly sailed away. He left an order for Raleigh to follow him to Fayal, one of the smaller islands, and to join him there in an assault upon Horta, the island's port and capital.

Essex left no explanation of his sudden departure, which was caused by a rumour that the treasure convoy had been sighted. He raced off on a fruitless goose-chase. Raleigh duly anchored his squadron off Fayal, and waited three days for his chief to

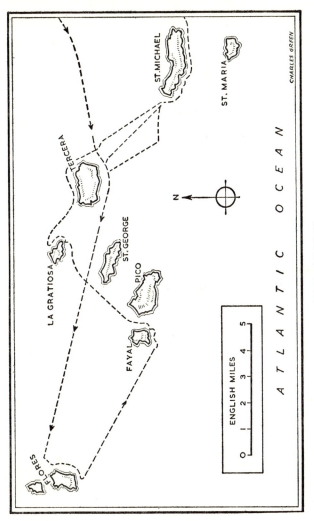

THE AZORES

ATLANTIC OCEAN

ST. MICHAEL

ST. MARIA

TERCERA

LA GRATIOSA

ST. GEORGE

PICO

FAYAL

FLORES

N

ENGLISH MILES

0 1 2 3 4 5

CHARLES GREEN

arrive. He had to watch the enemy building entrenchments and making preparations for defence. His pride was troubled by the thought that the enemy believed that he did not dare to attack them, and on 21st September, 1597, he gave the order to disembark. The order did not apply to certain partisans of Essex who had represented that the Commander-in-Chief would be angry if he arrived to find that Raleigh had stolen from him the honour of storming the town:

' I landed those English in Fayal myself ', Raleigh wrote, in an incidental passage in the *History of the World*: '. . . Some in that voyage advised me not to undertake it; and I hearkened unto them somewhat longer than was requisite, especially when they desired me to reserve the title of such an exploit for a greater person. But when they began to tell me of " difficulty " I gave them to understand that it is more difficult to defend a coast than to invade it. The truth is, I could have landed my men with more ease than I did—yea, without finding any resisting, if I would have rowed to another place; yea, even there, where I landed if I would have taken more company to help me. But, without fearing any imputation of rashness, I may say that I had more regard to reputation in that business than to safety . . . And further, I was unwilling that some Low Country captains, and others, not of mine own squadron, whose assistance I had refused, should please themselves with the sweet conceit . . . that for want of their help I was driven to turn tail. Therefore I took with me none but men assured ... The enemy troubled us more in our march towards Fayal (Horta) than in our taking the shore.'

Raleigh's assault was brilliantly successful—the one effective incident of the campaign. He landed four miles from the town and led the assault on it himself; bullet-holes were found in his clothes when the place was finally stormed. The next morning, 22nd September, Essex's sails were seen by the victors off Horta.

Essex's partisans, whose services Raleigh had not utilized, now raced off to Essex, on his flagship. They represented that Raleigh's action had been designed only to steal from the Commander-in-Chief the honour and fame of the assault. There was no man living who was more greedy of fame than Essex, and he immediately summoned Raleigh to visit him on board the *Repulse*. He accused Raleigh of disobeying an order that no subordinate commander should land troops without authority, and asked him to state reasons why he should not be tried by court-martial.

Raleigh defended himself with adroitness. He claimed that the order that no subordinate commander should land troops without authority did not apply to him. He was a principal commander, and, as such, in a position to issue the necessary order. He claimed, further, that he was entitled to construe, in the way he had done, Essex's order to attack Horta, for he had had no means of knowing what might have happened to delay the Commander-in-Chief.

The breach was patched up by Thomas Howard, who persuaded Raleigh to apologize and Essex to agree to take no further action. The affair gradually subsided, and Essex and Raleigh exchanged dinners again on board their flagships. The fleet remained off the Azores until the middle of October, occupied in hunting prizes. A few were captured, the biggest by Raleigh, but the great treasure convoy missed the English fleet by a gap of about three hours' sailing. Escorted by eight galleons, it was sighted too late by four isolated English ships as it sailed majestically into the port of Angra, on the island of Terceira, which was commanded by an impregnable castle. It had finally been agreed, at a council of war, that an assault on Terceira would be an unjustifiable and suicidal risk. Essex wished to reverse that decision, but he was dissuaded from courting disaster.

The expedition had been badly mismanaged, and there was nothing more to be done, except to sail for home. On the day when the fleet began its homeward voyage, Philip II's last armada left Ferrol in an attempt to take advantage of the exposed condition in which England had been left. The armada had orders to seize Falmouth and to disembark an army there. Panic gripped Whitehall and the West of England. The militia was mustered, and frantic messages of recall were dispatched to Essex in the Azores. But a storm came once again

*Plate 5 Robert Devereux, 2nd Earl of Essex, by an unknown
artist, 1597*

SERO SED SERIO

Plate 6 Robert Cecil, 1st Earl of Salisbury.
Attributed to J. de Critz, 1602

to the rescue of the islanders, and Philip's fleet crept back to Ferrol just as Essex's fleet was straggling into Plymouth. Both countries were weary of war, and Philip died a few months later. Elizabeth still retained the strength and spirit to blaze into a tremendous passion over the negative results and mismanagement of the expedition. There was nothing to show for its huge expense except loss of reputation, and the nation had been exposed to great danger. Essex was received by the Queen with extreme disapprobation, and he retired, temporarily, from the Court; Raleigh was left with room to spread his branches, and with the opportunity to find better nourishment and support for his roots, if he could. None knew better than he how to display his branches to advantage. Few paid less attention to their roots.

II

The years 1598 to 1603 were to the unsuspecting Raleigh the most tranquil and agreeable of his life. He had reached the climax of his career and was a great figure in the land and famous throughout the world. During the past few years he had risen to his full stature, and until the end of the reign his star continued to rise as that of Essex declined and then, dramatically, set. He was rich, envied, and extremely influential. There was no more important political centre in London than Durham Palace, where Raleigh freely discussed coming events with his friends. He was still intensely unpopular, but his personality extorted involuntary admiration and respect. Great magnates, like the Earl of Northumberland, and Lord Cobham who was Sir Robert Cecil's brother-in-law, took him to their hearts at last, and paid public tribute to his character and abilities. They were, however, incapable politicians and of no account in the fast-developing struggle for power. Northumberland, moreover, proved to be false in friendship. Raleigh sensed, without in any way understanding, the mesh of intrigue which Cecil was weaving around him, and he strove to protect himself as best he could against it. He failed to see that Northumberland and Cobham were no better than glittering façades, and he lacked the true politician's instinct which would have enabled him to appreciate the position in which he stood.

He had certainly become an institution, and so long as the Queen lived his position was reasonably safe. He was, however, bitterly hated by the people; he was enormously wealthy; and his position was wholly dependent upon the Queen. There was never a better case for reaching out an arm towards the rising sun.

Raleigh's temperament made it natural for him to assume that the Spanish war would endure, and that the privateering business, with which he was so closely identified, would continue on the old terms. But with his experience of the world he ought to have been more cautious. He was too grand to realize until it was too late that Cecil was about to engage himself secretly in the cold-blooded work of poisoning the King of Scotland's mind against him. And he never appreciated the motives which prompted Cecil to behave in that way.

Cecil, who plumed himself upon his integrity, distrusted Raleigh's personal magnetism and unco-ordinated genius. Those incalculable qualities were antipathetic to him and outside his range of experience. He considered that Raleigh had been rewarded on a scale which vastly exceeded his worth, and he felt for his statesmanship and political instinct a full measure of the professional's contempt for the amateur. The King of Scotland, who was the Queen's unacknowledged heir, hated everything for which Raleigh stood—a forward policy, and endless war with Spain. Cecil could afford to despise Raleigh's belated attempt to buttress his position with the support of such men as Northumberland and Cobham; he resolved to play him with fair words and to be rid of him as soon as the time was ripe.

The most resounding event in the last years of the Queen's reign was the rebellion of Essex. His success and popularity had gone to his head, so that he became spoiled and in part unbalanced. He was ready to quarrel with anyone, including the Queen. On one occasion, when she boxed his ears, he called her to her face ' a King in petticoats '. Worse was to follow.

A rebellion had broken out in Ireland, and Essex

was sent to suppress it. He went over as Lord Deputy in March, 1599, but he temporized and negotiated with the rebels, instead of acting ruthlessly and promptly in order to save the Queen expense, as he had been told to do. Raleigh, from patriotic motives, was among the severest critics of Essex's conduct of the war in Ireland. Cecil, who had already secured a majority of his own supporters in the Privy Council, characteristically took advantage of Essex's absence to procure the dismissal of a devoted follower of Essex—Edward Hutton, Archbishop of York—from the post of Lord President of the Council of the North.

Hutton was at that moment a figure of great political importance in relation to the balance of power between Cecil and Essex at Court. He was replaced by Cecil's elder brother, the second Lord Burghley, who proceeded immediately to secure the North for the Cecil interest. Essex, who was already in touch with the Scottish King, and who was, in fact, at that moment his candidate for power, realized in a flash the significance of Cecil's underground intrigues. He had an important following of peers and gentry; he rejoiced in the knowledge that he was the darling of the mob; he rushed back from Ireland, accordingly, in September, 1599, in defiance of the Queen's order to remain at his post, and with the firm determination to settle accounts with his opponents.

When he reached London, Essex was placed under arrest and deprived of all his offices. The

Court was in a ferment, but public opinion, which idolized the handsome young patrician, was dangerously inflamed. Reluctantly, but with that instinctive understanding of the arts of popularity which always characterized her, Elizabeth, in February, 1600, cancelled the arrangements which had been made for Essex's trial. At that moment Raleigh wrote to Cecil:

' I am not wise enough to give you advice, but if you take it for a good counsel to relent towards this tyrant, you will repent it when it shall be too late. His malice is fixed and will not evaporate by any of your mild courses, for he will ascribe the alteration to Her Majesty's pusillanimity and not to your good nature. The less you make him, the less he shall be able to harm you and yours. And if Her Majesty's favour fail him, he will again decline to a common person. For after-revenges, fear them not; for your own father was esteemed to be the contriver of Norfolk's [1] ruin, yet his son followeth your father's son, and loveth him.'

Raleigh concluded:

' Lose not your advantage. If you do, I read your destiny.'

Essex, he asserted, was the ' canker ' of the Queen's life and realm.

That letter was certainly ruthless and cold-blooded; it reads like a plea for Essex's execution, and it was not a wise letter to send. Raleigh failed to appreciate that he had even more to fear from

[1] The fourth Duke of Norfolk had been executed in 1572.

Cecil than from Essex; and the Machiavellian advice which he gave might almost have been calculated to justify Cecil's determination to effect Raleigh's destruction as well as that of Essex. Furthermore, the suggestion that Essex could ever decline into ' a common person ' was absurd. It is just possible that Raleigh was deliberately using the kind of arguments which he thought would appeal most to Cecil, but he did not share Cecil's understanding of the way in which the Queen's feelings towards Essex were precariously balanced. She hated and adored him at the same time, and Cecil would have been mad to attempt to influence her decision. He wanted Essex's head, but if he had pressed for his execution he would either have failed, or else have incurred the Queen's bitterest resentment as the price of success.

Cecil, therefore, bided his time, and Essex regained his freedom. He was, however, forbidden the Court, and during the months which followed the acid of frustration bit deeply into his mind. He resolved to stake everything on a *coup d'état* aimed at turning out the old gang in Whitehall. He sent envoys secretly to the Scottish King and to Lord Mountjoy (formerly Sir Charles Blount) who had taken over the command in Ireland, and he calculated on using his great personal popularity to raise the City against the Queen, to capture the Court, and to dictate his terms. His conspiracy was hatched during the first week of February, 1601, at Drury House, in the Strand, the residence of Essex's friend and supporter, the Earl of Southampton. With superb patrician insolence, the two Earls made Shakespeare's company stage at the Globe Theatre during that week a performance of *Richard II.* Rumour declared at once that Essex was planning to repeat Bolingbroke's action in deposing his Sovereign, and Essex himself spread a report that Raleigh and Cobham were planning to assassinate him.

On Saturday, 7th February, 1601, Essex was summoned to appear before the Privy Council, but he pleaded illness. Early on the Sunday morning, Raleigh ordered his cousin, Sir Ferdinand Gorges, who was one of Essex's devoted followers, to report to him at Durham House. Sir Ferdinand, who as Governor of Plymouth was Raleigh's subordinate officer, agreed to meet Raleigh in a boat on the Thames, shortly before three of the most important members of the Privy Council—the Earl of Worcester (Lord Keeper), Sir John Popham (Chief Justice), and Sir William Knollys (Controller)— called at Essex House. They had orders to demand in the Queen's name to know the meaning of recent assemblies and actions on the part of Essex, Southampton, and their friends, which had caused confusion and aroused suspicion.

When Raleigh's boat drew alongside that of Gorges, opposite Essex House, Raleigh coldly remarked that he held a warrant for Gorges's arrest. He ordered Gorges to return immediately to Plymouth and to await developments there. Gorges warned Raleigh that two thousand gentlemen were resolved that day to obey the orders of Essex and ' to live or die as free men.' At that moment one of Essex's followers on the riverside aimed four shots at Raleigh with a musket, and a boat, filled with musketeers, put off from Essex Stairs.

The shots which had been aimed at Raleigh went wide, and while Gorges returned to Essex House, Raleigh had himself rowed to Whitehall. Shortly afterwards the Privy Councillors, whom the Queen had sent to Essex House, demanded entrance. They were duly admitted but were at once informed that they must regard themselves as prisoners.

The die was cast, and at the head of two or three hundred men-at-arms, Essex rode along the Strand into the City. He called upon the citizens to rise and to protect the Queen and himself from traitors and pro-Spaniards in disguise. There was no response and he was greeted with silence, amazement, and alarm.

The Government acted with promptness and decision. Essex was proclaimed a traitor and barricades were erected in the principal streets. In danger of being cut off, Essex recollected his hostages at Essex House, to which he returned by river. He found that the prisoners had been released by one of his more timid followers, and within a short time Essex House was surrounded by loyal troops.

Cannon were brought to bear and after a few rounds had been fired Essex was compelled to surrender. He was tried for treason, sentenced, and

beheaded on 25th February, 1601. Five of his principal supporters suffered death, but Southampton,
who was also sentenced, was reprieved.

Essex was only thirty-three when he died, ack-
nowledging on the scaffold that he was being ' justly
spewed out of the realm.' Raleigh, as Captain of
the Guard, should have been present when the
great axe fell. He had, however, excused himself
because he had been accused by the rabble, as well
as by Essex, of thirsting for Essex's blood. He
watched the scene from a distant window in the
Armoury, and he did not know that Essex had
demanded on the scaffold to know where he was
and that he had expressed a wish for reconciliation.
It was a matter of lasting regret to Raleigh that he
had missed that final opportunity.

In later years, Raleigh used to maintain that one
cruel speech by Essex had done even more to cost
him his head than his childish and futile rebellion.
He had forced his way into the Queen's presence
after his return from Ireland, and had refused to
listen while she attempted to lay down a few sensible
conditions to guide his future conduct. He had so
far taken leave of his senses as to tell the Sovereign
who loved him and who had borne with him so
long and so patiently that her conditions were as
crooked as her ancient carcass.

In the world's eyes Raleigh gained greatly as a
result of Essex's fall, and he thereby incurred further
odium. It was, however, Cecil who reaped all the
benefit. He received the Scottish King's secret

envoys when they reached London in response to the invitation which Essex had sent, and he reached a complete understanding with them. By that superb and characteristic stroke of diplomatic finesse, Cecil secured his own future and sealed the fate of Raleigh.

After the death of Essex, the Queen began to employ Raleigh in an ever-widening circle of public duties; and his natural complacency was proportionately increased. His enemies were giving ground; he was not yet 50; there was time for the Privy Council, the Peerage, and much besides. It was a relief to be able to drop the courtly convention of romantic love between himself and his aged Sovereign. He had become to her a habit, and he felt proud and confident of the future. The Scottish King would presumably succeed Elizabeth; his friend, Cecil, would see to that; James would feel very strange when he first arrived in Whitehall. What could be more natural than that the new King should turn at once to those upon whom the Queen had depended? He had only to bide his time, and all would fall into his lap.

So he took the waters at Bath, and enjoyed at Sherborne, in the beautiful gardens which he had planned, the society of his wife and young son, Walter, who had been born in 1594. Lady Raleigh, who had been permanently forbidden the Court, had come to love Sherborne better than anywhere else. The treacherous Cecil was a frequent visitor there. At intervals Raleigh attended more frequently to his duties in the House of Commons, where he had first represented Devon, and, later, Cornwall. He made an eloquent speech on 20th November, 1601, in defence of monopolies, which were very unpopular. He himself enjoyed valuable monopolies in tin, wine, and playing-cards. An eye-witness said that when he sat down ' there was a great silence '; the ballad-makers lampooned him:

Raleigh doth time bestride;
He sits 'twixt wind and tide,
Yet uphill he cannot ride,
For all his bloody pride.
He seeks taxes in the tin;
He polls the poor to the skin;
Yet he swears 'tis no sin!

In opposition to Cecil, however, Raleigh urged the repeal of the duties on corn. Cecil replied that whoever failed to maintain the plough would ruin the kingdom.

In September, 1600, Raleigh was appointed Governor of Jersey, a post which he found less lucrative than he had expected. He set out from Weymouth where ' little Wat ', his son, remained with Lady Raleigh and Cecil's boy, Will, enjoying the sea-bathing. Raleigh liked Jersey, where he instituted reforms and abolished a number of sine-cures, but he did not spend long periods on it. He was very restless. He spent too much time with Lord Cobham, Lord Warden of the Cinque Ports and a Knight of the Garter, who was wealthy and amusing, but a weak character. Cobham was constantly at Durham Palace, and Cecil noted dryly that the two flitted over to France together to see war again at close quarters for the last time, since they had become convinced that the Queen, unfortunately, was becoming eager to put a stop to the war. That friendship with Cecil's brother-in-law was almost Raleigh's sole insurance policy against the risk that Cecil might prove treacherous. As such it proved worthless, and it was, in fact, the immediate cause of Raleigh's ruin.

There were rumours that Raleigh was to be sworn off the Privy Council and promoted to the House of Lords, but Cecil, while outwardly professing warm friendship, blocked every move towards either of those ends. Raleigh was, however, employed constantly in a diplomatic capacity. He received foreign envoys and distinguished visitors, and did them the honours of the Court and Capital. The Duke of Sully, the great French statesman, recorded in his Memoirs, that soon after he had entered his room at Dover, on his way to London, Raleigh approached him, jocularly, while his back was turned, with the words: ' I arrest you as my prisoner, in the Queen's name.'

' It was ', Sully records, ' the Captain of her Guard, whose embrace I returned, telling him I should consider such an imprisonment as a great honour.'

Spanish envoys were also among the distinguished visitors entertained by Raleigh at that time.

Raleigh had failed to make himself indispensable, and his position was, therefore, fundamentally unsound. He was brilliant, versatile, sinister, fascinating; but to many he seemed a magnificent and expensive luxury. Cecil was confident of his own indispensability, but the Scottish King, with whom he had entered into close and secret relations, was romantic, impressionable, unpredictable. He was certain to be governed by favourites who were likely to be rapacious Scots. They would require careful management, and Raleigh's great possessions might contribute something towards satisfying their needs.

Cecil watched Raleigh narrowly, made his plans, and kept his counsel, while Raleigh suspected little or nothing. His temperament was that of a soldier of fortune, and warfare was his element, by sea or land. From that element he had been lifted by the chance of his Sovereign's whim, and for years he had revelled in his good fortune. But that fortune had made him an object of envy, hatred and distrust. It never once occurred to him that it might be wise to conciliate those feelings, and he was appallingly complacent. Even Essex had seen the necessity of entering into secret correspondence with the Scottish King, but Raleigh made no move to secure himself in that all-important quarter. He relied on such men as Northumberland and Cobham who loomed large in the eyes of the man in the street, but who were, in fact, without influence. Above all he grossly underestimated the possibility of personal treachery such as that which Cecil employed.

Cecil lied shamelessly to the Scottish King about Raleigh. He said that Raleigh hated the prospect of coming under his rule. He played upon the King's religious bigotry by representing Raleigh as ' one that denies the Trinity ', and as ' a person that all religious men do hold anathema.'

Raleigh was never particularly discreet, and the slightest gossip about him was retailed to King James with a great air of solemnity. His friend, Lord Cobham, was equally unguarded in his speech, and Cecil detested his brother-in-law, whose name was constantly coupled with that of Raleigh. He alleged that they had discussed forcing terms upon James in regard to the number of Scotsmen whom he should be allowed to bring with him into England. He alleged further that Raleigh had expressed regret that a commonwealth could not be established after the Queen's death, in order to save the English from the indignity of being ruled by a gang of beggarly Scots. Lord Henry Howard, Cecil's close ally in that secret correspondence, had always disliked Raleigh. He wrote to King James's agent, Lord Mar, that the Earl of Nottingham (formerly Lord Howard of Effingham) ' the other day wished from his soul that he had the same commission to carry the cannon to Durham House that he had this time twelve months to carry it to Essex House.'

In a short time James's mind was completely poisoned, and all the while Cecil was careful to send

Raleigh frequent assurances of his affection and regard.

Queen Elizabeth died on 24th March, 1603; King James I was proclaimed on the same day. A further proclamation was issued forbidding unauthorized persons from seeking audience while the King, showering knighthoods right and left, was on his journey to London. Raleigh had been in Devon when the Queen died, but he was used to coming and going as he pleased. Unsuspecting, he hastened to meet his new Sovereign, and is said to have been greeted with the atrocious pun:

' Rawley! Rawley! True enough, for I think of thee rawly, mon! '

Cecil was at once informed that Raleigh had ' failed to take root '. He was forbidden further access and was shortly afterwards deprived of his cherished office of Captain of the Guard. He was handsomely compensated, but the storm clouds gathered rapidly. On 31st May he was ordered to quit Durham Palace within three weeks, so that it could be restored to the Bishop of Durham. Still he failed to understand. He was sometimes extraordinarily insensitive. With great want of tact he prepared and sent to the King a memorandum on the Spanish war, which contained, amongst other proposals, a plan for the conquest of the West Indies. And yet he must have known that James was bent on peace. He prepared a written protest against his dismissal from the Captaincy of the Guard, in which he accused Cecil of prejudicing James's mind

against him; but a month later, just before he was
arrested, he referred, in a letter to his wife, to the
old privateering partnership between himself and
Cecil as though it were still a live and friendly asso-
ciation.

That letter was, in fact, less surprising than it
might appear; for Cecil had continued from time
to time to take shares on the old basis in Raleigh's
joint-stock expeditions. He did so only in order to
lull Raleigh's suspicions, and he was careful to
cover himself with King James. The storm burst
over Raleigh's head during the second week of
July, 1603. He was confined to his house under
open arrest on suspicion of being involved in treason.

* 5 *

Years of Suspense

R ALEIGH'S TRIAL, which aroused tremendous controversy, has not contributed to the fame of
British criminal justice. His light-hearted habits of
speech and conduct were in part responsible for his
fall, but generations of lawyers, after examining the
evidence, have condemned equally the manner in
which the trial was conducted and the verdict.
Raleigh was so self-confident and so accustomed to
despise his enemies that he rode headlong into the
pit. He regarded himself as fortune's favourite.
He could not conceive that, even in the case of
someone as envied, unpopular, and mistrusted as
himself, it was necessary to take elementary precautions in case his words or actions should be mis-
construed.

During Elizabeth's last years, when men's minds
were troubled about the succession, anarchy was as
much dreaded as the plague. The fulsome terms of
flattery which the anonymous authors of the Auth-
orized Version of the Bible used in dedicating their
work to James I is a measure of the relief felt by all

classes of Englishmen when the transition had been
peacefully accomplished. But as the old reign
closed and the new one opened there was an epidemic
of plots, which culminated in 1605, two years after
James's accession, in the attempt of Guy Fawkes
and a group of Roman Catholic gentlemen to blow
up the King and both Houses of Parliament at once.

The plot in which Raleigh found himself en-
meshed was hatched soon after James's accession.
Lord Cobham, and his younger brother, George
Brooke, were concerned, with others, in a foolish
conspiracy to kidnap the King at Greenwich, and
in vague treasonable conversations with Count
Arenberg, Ambassador in London from the Arch-
duke Charles, the nominee of Spain to the throne
of the Netherlands. The presumed objects were to
substitute Lady Arabella Stuart for James on the
throne, to secure peace with Spain, toleration for
Catholics, and personal advantage. There was
never any chance of success, for the conspirators
mistrusted and betrayed each other. They were,
moreover, undecided and half-hearted, and Cecil,
who was master of the situation, held most of the
threads in his hands.

Arabella Stuart was the great-granddaughter of
Henry VIII's sister, Margaret, and a cousin of
King James. She was never more than an innocent
tool, but Arenberg made successful approaches to
Cobham, and Raleigh was cognizant of them. As
an inflexible opponent of peace with Spain, Raleigh
lent a ready and amused ear to Cobham's wild talk

about the conspiracy; but he declined to take part in it and awoke too late to the desperate nature of his position.

Raleigh's silence was justly construed in law as tantamount to consent, and Raleigh was shrewd enough to have appreciated from the outset that this must be so. He was betrayed, however, by a fantastic pride. A man accused of treason at that time was required to prove his innocence; and Raleigh could never hope to do that. He considered, however, that he was morally innocent, because he had declined to take part in any conspiracy. After Cobham and his brother, George Brooke, had been arrested with other conspirators early in July, 1603, Raleigh was summoned before the Council and invited to explain his conduct. Although well aware of Cobham's guilt, Raleigh denied all knowledge of guilty communications. That lie was fatal, but he wrote at once to tell Cobham that he had cleared him.

Cecil, who knew all the relevant facts, understood Raleigh's predicament. As far as his nature and conscience permitted, he felt some sympathy with Raleigh, who realised at last how madly he had behaved and how hopelessly he had compromised himself. As soon as he was told that Cobham had confessed his guilt, Raleigh suffered a traumatic shock. He admitted impulsively that he had lied to the Council, and decided that his sole chance was to throw himself upon Cecil's mercy. He wrote, accordingly, to inform Cecil that he had in fact been aware for some time that Cobham had been in communication with Arenberg, and he even named a foreign agent who had served as intermediary. He insisted, nevertheless, that he had regarded the affair from start to finish as a childish prank which did not deserve the notice of serious and responsible men; and that his knowledge, such as it was, had been very loose and imperfect.

The conspirators were in a mood to say anything which offered a chance of saving their necks. They were interrogated daily and nightly, and on 20th July Cobham was shown the letter which Raleigh had written to Cecil. Assuming that Raleigh had betrayed and denounced him in the first instance, Cobham in turn denounced Raleigh, exclaiming: ' O traitor! O villain! I will now tell you the truth.'

He said that Raleigh had instigated the negotiation with Arenberg, and that Arenberg had offered half a million crowns for distribution to malcontents in England. Raleigh had previously been subject only to house arrest. He was at once committed to the Tower and formally charged with treason. Raleigh felt himself then to be surrounded by bitter enemies intent on his destruction, and for a moment his courage failed him. He tried to commit suicide by stabbing himself with a knife in the right breast. He inflicted a painful but not serious wound, which healed within a fortnight. In the meantime Cobham withdrew his charge against Raleigh. With the aid of friends Raleigh secured a formal letter from Cobham to that effect.

His courage revived, and he concealed the letter. He had, however, to stand his trial for treason.

The trial opened on 17th November, 1603. It was held at Winchester on account of an outbreak of plague in London. During his journey from London to Winchester mobs gathered at every stage to insult and execrate the prisoner; and at times Raleigh's guards had difficulty in saving him from being lynched. The people's pent-up hatred and envy seemed to burst out in a flood of anger which threatened to overwhelm Raleigh, but his pride rose to meet the threat. He carried himself superbly and took every occasion to manifest the contempt which he felt for those who shouted against him. At the last moment, before the trial opened, the wretched Cobham, who was completely un-manned, wrote again to the Council reaffirming his charges against Raleigh. Raleigh was unaware of that, but he carried Cobham's letter of retraction in his pocket.

The trial was held before a jury by a mixed commission of professional and lay judges—a procedure which has no counterpart in similar trials to-day. Cecil, and Lord Thomas Howard (Earl of Suffolk), Raleigh's old comrade at Cadiz, were among the judges. The prosecution was directed and, in large part, conducted by Sir Edward Coke, the Attorney-General, who had prosecuted Essex and South-ampton. Coke's name is probably the greatest in the history of the Common Law, but he was a bully by nature and consumed by ambition; he was fully

resolved to secure a conviction. The long indict-
ment charged Raleigh with conspiring to obtain
money through Arenberg for the purpose of sub-
verting the Government and the cause of true religion, and of advancing Arabella Stuart to the throne.
He pleaded ' not guilty '.

By the custom of the time Raleigh was required to
conduct his own defence, and he was not allowed to
call or question witnesses. In effect the trial became
a duel between Coke, who was an experienced
expert, and Raleigh, who knew little or nothing of
the law. It took the form of a dialogue which often
became impassioned. Coke discoursed pedantically
about the different phases of treason—the root, the
bud, the blossom, and the fruit; and he went on
to praise what he termed the sweetness and innocence of the King's nature. Raleigh impatiently
tried to recall him to the point, and Coke burst
out:

' I will prove all. Thou art a monster! Thou hast
an English face, but a Spanish heart.'

It was ludicrous to accuse Raleigh, of all men, of
possessing a ' Spanish heart ', and it was insulting
at that period to use the familiar forms, ' thou ' and
' thy ' in speaking to a stranger; but Coke's object
was to infuriate Raleigh and to discredit him before
the jury:

' I *thou* thee, thou traitor! I will prove thee the
rankest traitor in all England.'

Coke described Raleigh as a notorious atheist,
and after outlining the nature of Cobham's treason,

argued that no such diabolical invention could have come from Cobham's feeble intellect without Raleigh's assistance. Raleigh was quick to seize upon the weakness of that argument. He pointed out that Coke had failed to prove anything:

' If my Lord Cobham be a traitor, what is that to *me*? '

' All that he did ', Coke retorted, ' was by thy instigation.'

He continued to insult the prisoner, and then asked, eagerly:

' Have I angered you? '

' I am in no case to be angry ', was Raleigh's dignified rejoinder. Popham, the Chief Justice, called on both parties to remain calm. Coke concluded by reading aloud Cobham's original deposition charging Raleigh with being the instigator of his treason.

In his defence Raleigh argued with force and spirit that he had fought against Spain all his life. It was therefore inconceivable that he could ever wish to conspire with a man of straw, like Cobham, on behalf of an exhausted and impoverished enemy, at a time when England had never been stronger or more united. England, he pointed out, was now governed by an active King, in place of ' a lady whom time had surprised '. That beautiful phrase was characteristic, and made an impression. He argued that the case against him depended entirely on the word of one man—Cobham. He said that, in the case of treason, two witnesses were necessary to secure a conviction, but the lawyers retorted that there was plenty of evidence. He asked that he should be confronted in Court by Cobham, but that, too, was refused, although Cecil appeared to think the request a reasonable one. The majority of the judges were afraid that Raleigh's powerful personality would cause Cobham to withdraw a statement which incriminated himself as well as Raleigh. One piece of evidence admitted against Raleigh was the story of an English pilot, who had heard an unknown person say in Lisbon that the King of England's throat would be cut by Raleigh and Cobham.

' What infer you upon that? ' Raleigh demanded.

' That your treason hath wings ', Coke retorted.

It seems certain that Coke was convinced of Raleigh's guilt, but Cecil seems on more than one occasion to have felt qualms during the trial. At one point he said to Coke:

' Be not so impatient, Master Attorney. Give him leave to speak.'

Coke was so offended that he sat down, and had to be coaxed by the other judges before he would consent to continue. He warned Cecil against encouraging traitors. On another occasion Cecil called uneasily to Raleigh:

' Excepting your fault, I am your friend.'

He had previously declared that he loved Raleigh, and felt a great conflict within himself.

While Coke was recapitulating the evidence, the following exchange took place:

COKE: ' Thou are the most vile and execrable traitor that ever lived.'

RALEIGH: ' You speak indiscreetly, barbarously, and uncivilly.'

COKE: ' I want words to express thy viperish treason.'

RALEIGH: ' I think you want words indeed, for you have spoken one thing half a dozen times.'

COKE: ' Thou art an odious fellow. Thy name is hateful to all the realm of England for thy pride.'

RALEIGH: ' It will go near to prove a measuring-cast between you and me, Mr. Attorney.'

Immediately before the end, Coke warned the jury that the King's safety depended upon Raleigh's conviction, and he laid a trump card on the table. It was a fresh letter written by Lord Cobham to the Council on the previous day, in which Raleigh was accused of trying to procure a pension for Cobham from Spain in return for a promise to reveal to Spanish agents plans of any future military or naval operations. That letter was a shattering blow to Raleigh, for it seemed to deprive his own letter from Cobham, which had been written earlier, of most of its force. It was, however, his last card, and he therefore exposed it to the Court; but Coke claimed that the letter to the Council was much more valuable, since Cobham, in writing it, had incriminated himself, as well as Raleigh. Cobham was, in fact, yielding to an impulse common to all accused persons of weak character who believe themselves to be guilty. Such people hope, by means of confessions, to mitigate their punishments by engaging the sympathy of their judges. So long as they hope to attain that object they are careless whether what they say is true or false.

' What say you now to the letter? ' Coke asked, referring to Lord Cobham's letter to the Council of the previous day.

' I say that Cobham is a base, dishonourable, poor soul.'

' Is he base? I return it in thy throat on his behalf. But for thee he would have been a good subject.'

Raleigh made a last appeal to the jury, begging them to remember that Cobham, in writing to him, had sworn on his faith as a Christian, whereas in writing to the Council he had taken no oath. He must have felt, as he said that, that he was beaten. The jury were absent only fifteen minutes, and they returned a verdict of ' guilty '. Raleigh threw himself on the King's mercy, complained of his unjust usage, and was sentenced to be hanged, drawn, and quartered.

' I never saw the like trial ', the Chief Justice declared in passing sentence, ' and I hope I shall never see the like again.'

Another of the professional judges, Gaudy, on his deathbed declared that the trial had degraded English justice. But Raleigh's noble bearing and the widespread fear that he had been unjustly condemned, precipitated a powerful reaction of feeling in his favour. ' Never ', wrote Sir Dudley Carleton, ' was a man so hated and so popular in so short a time.' It was said that many who would have travelled a hundred miles before his trial to see him hanged would have gladly travelled a thousand to save him when it was ended.

The trial of the other accused conspirators followed, and the verdicts were the same. Cobham was abject in Court. ' Never ', wrote Carleton, ' was there so poor and abject a spirit.' There can be little doubt about his substantial guilt. Raleigh, in prison, faced with the prospect of a traitor's death, wrote grovelling letters to the King, to Cecil, and to others, begging for mercy. But his courage quickly revived, and he grew ashamed of what he had done. He wrote to his wife from the gaol at Winchester on 9th December, 1603:

' Get those letters, if it be possible, which I writ to the Lords, wherein I sued for my life. God knoweth that it was for you and yours that I desired it, but it is true that I disdain myself for begging it. And know, dear wife, that your son is the child of a true man, who, in his own respect, despises death in all his misshapen and ugly forms.'

He begged her to secure his body and to have it buried at Sherborne, if possible, or if not in the Cathedral at Exeter by the graves of his parents. As for the rest:

' I beseech you for the love you bare me living, that you do not hide yourself many days, but by your travail seek to help your miserable fortunes, and the right of your poor child. Your mourning cannot avail me that am but dust . . .

'. . . I trust that my blood will quench their malice that desire my slaughter, and that they will not also seek to kill you and yours by extreme poverty. To what friend to direct thee I know not, for all have left me in the true time of trial; and I plainly perceive that my death was determined from the first day. Most sorry I am (as God knoweth) that, being thus surprised by death, I can leave you no better estate . . . If you can live free from want, care for no more, for the rest is vanity . . .

'. . . When I am gone no doubt you shall be sought unto by many, for the world thinks that I was very rich. But take heed of the pretences of men, and of their affections . . . I speak it (God knoweth) not to dissuade you from marriage, for that will be best for you . . . As for me, I am no more yours, nor you mine. Death hath cut us asunder, and God hath divided me from the world, and you from me.

' Remember your poor child for his father's sake that chose you and loved you in his happiest time . . .

' I cannot write much. God knows how hardly I stole this time, when all sleep; and it is time to separate my thoughts from the world . . . Time and death call me away . . .'

But in Raleigh's case the King enjoyed a measure of control over time and death; he was prevailed upon to suspend their summons for fifteen years.

II

The trial had not gone according to plan, and the reaction in Raleigh's favour was as disconcerting as it was unexpected. James was well aware of the English passion for fair play, and he was not prepared to face the odium of giving effect, at any rate at that time, to what many regarded as an unjust sentence. The Queen (Anne of Denmark) and Lady Pembroke, with several members of the Council, interceded on Raleigh's behalf. Two Catholic priests were hanged on 29th November, 1603, and on 5th December George Brooke, Cobham's brother, was beheaded; 10th December was the date fixed for the execution of Cobham, and two others; Raleigh's death was to follow three days later.

On 10 December Cobham was led to the scaffold with two other condemned men (his sentence had been commuted from hanging to decapitation). Of those three, Cobham alone had been told that he was not to die, and that the proceedings were, in fact, a farce. He was the first to mount the scaffold, where he confessed his guilt with a cheerful countenance, and repeated his accusation against Raleigh. The King's mercy was then publicly proclaimed. He was taken back to gaol, with his fellow-prisoners, who had each had to go through the same performance. Thence they were removed to the Tower where Cobham remained until 1617, when he was released, on leave, to die. One of his two fellow-prisoners died in the Tower; the other died abroad, in exile, while serving as a spy for Cecil. For three days Raleigh was uncertain whether he would be reprieved or not. As soon as he was informed of the King's mercy, he wrote suitable letters of thanks to the King and to Cecil. He told Cecil:

' I have failed both in friendship and in judgment. Therefore this is all that I can now say for myself: vouchsafe to esteem me as a man raised from the dead, though not in body, yet in mind.'

He begged that he might be allowed to retain some portion of his estate, which was forfeited automatically by his attainder:

' Of £3,000 a year there remains but £300, and upon that, £3,000 debt.' He was utterly ruined, and Cecil, in response to repeated appeals by Lady Raleigh, was, in the end, unexpectedly generous.

After his sentence was suspended Raleigh was removed to the Tower, where his imprisonment was, on the whole, made as easy for him as possible. The Governor was friendly, and at once allowed his prisoner the use of his private garden. Raleigh dined with him often, and many friends came to visit him. The quarters allotted to Raleigh were changed occasionally, but they were never disagreeable, and Lady Raleigh sometimes shared them. She took a house on Tower Hill, where their second son, Carew, was born in 1605. Raleigh was, however, at times subjected to periods of restraint, which he bitterly resented. Governors changed, and the authorities were at first dismayed by his habit of parading at fixed times before sight-seers on the wall of the small garden he had made. He was often applauded, and he became such a popular institution, that the public almost ceased to be interested in the lions which were kept in the Tower. They flocked there instead on the chance of catching a glimpse of Sir Walter Raleigh. It became known that he had fitted up a small labora-tory, where he conducted chemical experiments. He was helped by his friend, Thomas Hariot, the foremost scientist of the day, as well as by the more superficial Earl of Northumberland. It was believed that he was trying to produce elixirs containing mar-vellous properties. He issued pills and other medi-cines, and in effect, he turned the Tower into a university. The mob was ready to acclaim him as a magician, and the great world was fascinated. The Prince of Wales, a bright, lively youth in his teens, conceived a romantic infatuation for Raleigh, on which the prisoner naturally built high hopes. The Prince visited him a great deal, and listened spellbound to his stories. He is said to have re-marked:

' No one but my father would keep such a bird in a cage! '

The Queen, too, was friendly and well disposed, and in the course of time Raleigh's personality came to dominate the Tower. His pride and cour-age burned as brightly as they had done in his most prosperous days. He nearly always had a garden and a gallery for his private use, and quarters which were fit to receive visitors. He refused, in spite of all rebuffs, to act like a man dead in the eyes of the law. His views and comments on public affairs were eagerly sought and widely circulated.

Before his trial Raleigh had transferred his favourite estate at Sherborne to his elder son, reserving to himself a life interest. That interest was forfeited by his attainder, with the rest of his worldly possessions. But at that point Cecil intervened. He arranged that the income from Sherborne, and from certain other properties, should be assigned to trustees who would pay the income to Lady Raleigh. The conveyance was, however, carelessly drafted, and Raleigh was constantly writing letters in an attempt to mitigate the financial consequences of his attainder. Lady Raleigh was indefatigable; she laid siege to the Queen, and to Cecil (who became Earl of Salisbury in 1605), and would never take ' no ' for an answer. Sherborne was lost in the end, but some limited compensation was forthcoming.

Sherborne was lost because it was coveted by Robert Carr (Earl of Somerset), the King's reigning favourite before the all-conquering Buckingham appeared. In 1608 Raleigh wrote pathetically, but unavailingly, to Carr:

' After many great losses, and many years' sorrows . . . there remaineth nothing with me but the bare name of life . . . Your name is but in the dawn, and mine come to evening. I beseech you not to begin your first buildings upon the ruins of the innocent . . . that you will not be the first that will kill us outright, cut down the tree with the fruit, and undergo the curse of them that enter the fields of the fatherless . . .'

Although Carr grabbed Sherborne, he did not retain it very long. The Prince of Wales induced his father to allow him to acquire the place in return for the payment of a sum of over £20,000 to the favourite. The Prince hoped that one day it would be in his power to return the place to Raleigh's family, as soon as his friend's unhappy status as a man dead in law could be set right. The comfort of public sympathy was a new experience for Raleigh, but he valued it almost as little as he had formerly minded the world's dislike. He was self-contained, and when he needed occupation he took up his pen, not so much because he wanted to publish his opinions to the world, as in order to amuse himself and to instruct the Prince of Wales.

Raleigh's voluminous prose writings were mostly published after his death. They fall into four distinct groups of subjects. There were papers on current political issues, on political philosophy, and on ships and naval affairs. There were finally the historical writings, including the famous *History of the World*. The essays on current politics had the avowed aim of turning the Prince's mind away from his father's pro-Spanish policy. Raleigh cannot have known, although he may have suspected, that after peace was made with Spain in 1604, no less than four of his judges, including Cecil, had accepted secret pensions from Spain as a reward for pursuing a pro-Spanish policy.

Raleigh's prose works, like his actions, afford proof of his astonishing versatility. He expressed his views freely not only about matters of which he had expert knowledge, such as ship-building, and naval tactics, but about all subjects which aroused his interest, including religion and metaphysics. He was sometimes highly original, as when, in his *Prerogative of Parliaments*, he wrote that King John had been wronged when he was compelled against his will to sign Magna Carta.

Raleigh's greatest work, the *History of the World*, was published in 1614, and it achieved a wide popularity. It is a splendid torso, which carries the story from the Creation to 130 B.C. Nothing could have been more characteristically magnificent than Raleigh's action in sitting down cheerfully as a man, ruined, disgraced, and imprisoned, to write such a work. Its title is a measure of the boundless ambition and contempt for difficulties which were the hallmarks of all true Elizabethan adventurers. James I, who was prejudiced, complained that Raleigh had been ' too saucy in censuring the acts of Princes '; but Oliver Cromwell, one generation later, considered that the value and interest of Raleigh's *History* were second only to those of the Bible.

The way in which Raleigh himself regarded the book was made clear in the preface:

' It was for the service of that inestimable Prince Henry, the successive hope, and one of the greatest of the Christian world, that I undertook this work. It pleased him to peruse some parts thereof, and to pardon what was amiss. It is now left to the world, without a master.'

The Prince had died, aged only nineteen, of typhoid fever in November, 1612, and his death was a dismal blow to Raleigh. He ended his preface, however, with a characteristically light-hearted flourish. He could not, he wrote, expect his readers to be ' more ungentle or uncourteous ' than others who had misread him in the past. However, ' had it been otherwise I should hardly have had this leisure to have made myself a fool in print.'

In writing his *History*, Raleigh was, of course, indebted to many friends for help and advice, but the work is stamped throughout with the vivid impress of his personality. It is a monument of contemporary learning, salted with good sense and manly feeling. It is redolent of the charm and dignity of the best seventeenth-century prose. Take, for example, the following famous passage on the subject of death:

' The Kings and Princes of the world have always laid before them the actions, but not the ends, of those great Ones which preceded them . . . *I have considered*, saith Solomon, *all the works that are under the sun, and behold, all is vanity and vexation of spirit:*

but who believes it, till Death tells it us? . . . It is therefore Death alone that can suddenly make man to know himself. He tells the proud and insolent, that they are but Abjects, and humbles them at the instant; makes them cry, complain, and repent, yea, even to hate their forepassed happiness. He takes the account of the rich and proves him a beggar; a naked beggar which hath interest in nothing but in the gravel that fills his mouth. He holds a glass before the eyes of the most beautiful, and makes them see their deformity and rottenness; and they acknowledge it.

' O eloquent, just, and mighty Death! Whom none could advise, thou hast persuaded; what none hath dared thou hast done; and whom all the world hath flattered, thou only hast cast out of the world and despised. Thou hast drawn together all the far-stretched greatness, all the pride, cruelty, and ambition of man, and covered it all over with these two narrow words—*Hic Jacet.*'

Throughout all those years in the Tower, Raleigh never ceased to agitate for his release. He made use of the Queen, and of the Queen's brother, the King of Denmark, as well as of the Prince of Wales. The death of Cecil (Lord Salisbury) in 1612 counterbalanced, in some measure, that of the Prince of Wales. Cecil had been sold to Spain, but the new Secretary of State, Sir Ralph Winwood, saw eye to eye with Raleigh on public affairs. It was by a supreme triumph of personality that Raleigh, situated as he was, and with no ground to stand on whatsoever, should still have been able to make his influence so widely and powerfully felt. He used such modest funds as he was still able to command to bribe anyone who seemed likely to be of service. But his main lever continued to be the old plan of discovering treasure in Guiana, where fresh gold had been reported in 1609.

Raleigh's release was at last effected as a result of a temporary and accidental change caused by a shift in the balance of power at Court. Robert Carr, Earl of Somerset, and his wife, were disgraced in 1616 after the murder, by Lady Somerset, of Sir Thomas Overbury. Some of Somerset's enemies were anti-Spanish from patriotic motives, and they combined with others to influence the King to pursue a line of policy slightly more independent of Spain than that which he had hitherto followed. James reflected that if gold could be imported from Guiana, there was a chance that he might be made more independent of Parliament, which was beginning to grow very troublesome. It was but a slight and momentary shift in the way the wind blew, but it was sufficient to effect Raleigh's release. Spanish influence, in fact, was only mildly shaken, and Gondomar, the Spanish Ambassador, remained almost as powerful a figure at Court as before.

Even before Somerset's fall, young George Villiers, created Duke of Buckingham, had become the King's favourite. Raleigh bribed his two brothers with £750 apiece, and Villiers himself thereafter had a talk with the King. In March, 1616, the

Governor of the Tower received a warrant to release Raleigh in order that he might proceed overseas. He was told that he was ' to go abroad with a keeper ' [1] and warned not to attend the Court or to ' go into any public assemblies whatsoever '. A week after he had left the Tower, the Somersets moved in and took over the quarters he had left.

[1] Privy Council Minute, 19th March, 1616.

* 6 *

The Golden Fleece

Raleigh was aged sixty-four when he was released from the Tower, but his spirit was as youthful as ever. He still had, as Aubrey said, 'that awfulness and ascendancy in his aspect over other mortals'. His first act was to take a walk round London in order to see how much the place had changed in thirteen years. He was a founder of the long-lived Society of Antiquaries, and took a deep interest in such matters. He plunged with the greatest eagerness into the work of preparing his plans.

On 27th April, 1616, the Spanish Ambassador, Gondomar, wrote to his master, Philip III, about Raleigh's projected expedition. He said that he was doing all he could to stop it, and advised that the Spanish Fleet should be strengthened, and that no vessel should be allowed to sail except in convoy. The footing on which Gondomar's embassy was habitually conducted was illustrated in a letter of thanks which he wrote from Madrid in 1622 to the English King. He said that the fact that, while serving as Ambassador, he should have acted not merely as a member of King James's Privy Council but as an intimate of his Closet, exceeded not only any possible merit he could claim, but also all the value of all the services he could possibly have rendered. Gondomar's private estimate of James is also on record. He said that his vanity was so colossal that in order to govern him it was necessary to let him believe that anything said or done by the man with whom he was conversing was derived from the royal example. The Government of England was at that time to a very great extent controlled by James, his favourite 'George Villiers' who was an untried boy, and the subtle and gifted Gondomar.

Raleigh was fully conscious that he was being used as a pawn which would be sacrificed without hesitation if the game should require it. If he struck gold the King would find it useful, but, on the other hand, if the Spaniards could be induced to agree to a dynastic alliance between the future King Charles and one of their princesses, the expedition could be countermanded. There was an unbridgeable gulf between the spirit in which Raleigh embarked and the way in which the King and his advisers regarded the expedition. Raleigh was willing to dare all hazards in order to secure his release and re-establish his position. In answer to Gondomar's protest, he maintained that his mine was not on Spanish territory, but the responsibility of proving that was left with him. He was ordered to commit no outrages on Spanish subjects, but his temperament was well-known, and the Spanish

claim to the far distant and little-known territory
for which he was bound was never relinquished. It
was virtually certain that he would meet with a
hostile reception and that some clash on the spot
would occur. Raleigh's Commission left undefined
every important issue. As Admiral-in-Command
he had powers of life and death over his men. But
as a convicted traitor who had received no pardon
he himself remained dead in law, so that the situation was without precedent. There was precedent
only for the fact that the customary words ' trusty
and well-beloved ' were deliberately omitted from
his Commission; they had previously been omitted
when the Queen commissioned him to make his
first expedition to Guiana in 1595.

When Raleigh consulted Francis Bacon about the
propriety of embarking without a formal pardon,
he received the answer that his Commission was as
good a pardon for his former offences as the law
was capable of affording him. When Bacon went
on to ask Raleigh what he would do if he failed to
discover his mine, Raleigh replied:

' We will go for the Plate fleet.'

' But you will then be pirates.'

' Who ever heard of men being pirates for
millions! '

Such was the scornful rejoinder of the peer of
Drake, Grenville, and Hawkins, who had survived
into a less congenial age. It was a measure of the
difference in outlook between the Elizabethan and
the Jacobean worlds.

Gondomar realized from the first that Raleigh's expedition was irreconcilable with Spanish pretensions in South America. He renewed his protest, therefore, and was promised that if Raleigh interfered with Spanish subjects he would be handed over for public execution in Madrid. Although the dice were so heavily loaded against him, Raleigh could not accept his friends' advice to withdraw. Guiana was the dream and passion of his life. It gleamed before his eyes like the Golden Fleece, and beckoned him irresistibly forward. He was a stranger to caution, and he would have betrayed his own nature if he had withdrawn from a game which he loved so dearly and had been prevented from playing for so long. He deluded himself with the hope that the anti-Spanish faction at Court, led by Sir Ralph Winwood, the Secretary of State, would ultimately prevail. He could not know that Winwood would die within a year.

Before he started, Raleigh discussed with the Savoyard Ambassador an unformed project of seizing Genoa. Spain and Savoy were at war, and Genoa was then in Spanish hands. The Ambassador reported to the Duke of Savoy that he had found Raleigh eager to fall upon the Spaniards wherever he could, and to spare nothing Spanish, nor anything that depended on Spain. Raleigh listened cheerfully to private suggestions from the Savoyard and Venetian Ambassadors that he should enter the service of their countries, but without taking them seriously. He had listened previously, in much the same way, to Cobham. Situated as he was, however, and with his knowledge of the world, it was natural that Raleigh should think of taking elementary precautions in case his expedition should end in failure. Accordingly, when the French Ambassador put out private feelers to him, Raleigh indicated that in certain circumstances he might be willing to take service under the French flag. He complained of the bad usage he had had from his own Sovereign, and he accepted, as he admitted later, a Commission in the French Navy, for emergency use in case he should ever have occasion to take refuge in French territory.

Aided by loyal friends in Devon, Raleigh raised a joint-stock of thirty thousand pounds for his expedition, and a fleet of seven ships was built on the Thames. The essence of his plan was surprise. He intended the Spaniards to believe that he had reverted to his former love, and that he was planning an expedition to Virginia; he considered that King James betrayed him when he communicated all the details about the expedition to the Spanish Ambassador. In April, 1617, the little fleet sailed to Plymouth; the largest vessel, in which Raleigh flew his flag, was commanded by his son, Walter. It displaced 440 tons. The total force consisted of 431 men, including ninety gentlemen volunteers, with 121 pieces of ordnance. Young Walter Raleigh, after coming down from Oxford, had had the misfortune to kill a man in a brawl. Thereafter he had prudently spent some time abroad. He was boorish and wild, and Aubrey related an incident at a dinner-party at that time. Young Raleigh, in his cups, told an improper story at table, and was punished by his father with a box on the ears:

'His son, as rude as he was, would not strike his father, but strikes over the face of the gentleman that sat next to him, and said "box about; 'twill come to my father anon." 'Tis now a common used proverb.'

Among the gentlemen volunteers accompanying Raleigh's last expedition were his nephew, George Raleigh, and several dissipated and broken-down cadets of good family. Raleigh himself characterized his rank and file as the scum of the earth, but he had to be content with such rogues and cut-throats as he could find. On 12th June, 1617, the expedition put to sea; its commander had previously published a series of severe orders, for which in each case reasons were stated. Divine Service was to be read twice daily; there was to be no swearing, or drunkenness; women, and natives, were not to be molested.

Buffeted by gales the expedition put into Kinsale harbour on 3rd August, 1617. Lord Boyle, who had acquired Raleigh's former Irish properties, made good his diminished stores and entertained him well. The little fleet sailed again on 19th August, and put into two ports in the Canaries. At the first, great provocation was received from the Spaniards, but Raleigh restrained his men from retaliating.

Rumours reached England, nevertheless, that he had started already to indulge in piratical acts. At the second port, Gomora, Raleigh was treated with every courtesy, and the Governor wrote to Gondomar to say how well the English had behaved.

The ocean crossing to South America was exceedingly stormy, and when the coast of Guiana was sighted on 11th November, 1617, Raleigh and his second-in-command were both sick of a fever which had wasted the crews. Raleigh's nephew and namesake, George, together with the faithful Laurence Keymis, were therefore ordered to lead the party up the River Orinoco into the interior. Keymis had reported in 1596 on the location of the gold mine; since then the mine's existence had become fixed in Raleigh's mind as an article of faith. The orders given to the exploring party were to avoid hostile encounters, but to fight if attacked:

' I know ', he told Keymis, ' a few gentlemen excepted, what a scum of men you are. And I would not, for all the world, receive a blow from the Spaniards to the dishonour of our nation.'

That realistic view, taken by the man on the spot, was irreconcilable with that held in Whitehall about the necessity for avoiding a clash with the Spaniards. It had become clear that the Spaniards did not intend to stand aside while Raleigh's men explored for gold; they were now in effective control of territory which had been unoccupied twenty years before; and Raleigh was fully resolved that he would find his mine in defiance of any opposition that might be offered.

Keymis and young Raleigh went forward with the exploring party on 10th December, 1617, while Raleigh and the rest of the expedition sailed off to an agreed rendezvous off the coast of Trinidad. As the party made its way painfully up the River Orinoco it was at times harassed by small-arms fire from the banks; in due course it found a reception committee prepared to bar its further progress at the village of San Thomé, which had recently grown into a sizeable settlement. Keymis disembarked opposite that place on 2nd January, 1618, and was fired on by two mortars; he did not reply.

According to the spirit of the orders he had received Keymis ought at that juncture to have led his party through the forest to a point farther up-river, in order to avoid a clash. It was clear that San Thomé could not be entered without fighting. While he hesitated the Spaniards decided the question by sending a raiding party to attack the invaders during the night. There was a momentary panic, but young Walter Raleigh rallied his men, and drove the Spaniards back into the town. There they found the defenders drawn up in readiness, and at that critical moment Raleigh's son dashed forward to assault San Thomé. After a sharp fight the place was carried and the surviving Spaniards scattered into the surrounding country. But young Walter Raleigh fell mortally wounded during the brief engagement.

For a week Keymis idled at San Thomé, overcome by the untoward turn of events. He was encouraged a little by the discovery of miners' tools in the town. But the English were a demoralized party, and subsequent efforts made to find the mine were half-hearted. The Spaniards, after they had been driven from the town, ambushed the invaders wherever they went, and casualties were suffered and inflicted. San Thomé itself was virtually besieged. Raleigh's nephew, George, took a party a considerable distance up-river, but without achieving anything. When he returned, Keymis abandoned the search. He fired San Thomé, after plundering it, and sailed to his rendezvous with Raleigh off the coast of Trinidad. He arrived there on 2nd March, 1618.

Raleigh had already, on 14th February, 1618, heard from Keymis by letter of the fight at San Thomé and of the death in action of his son. He bitterly reproached Keymis, telling him that he had ruined him beyond hope of recovery, and that his return without striking gold after losing young Raleigh was unforgivable. He wrote to Winwood on 21st March, 1618, a full report of what had occurred:

' What shall become of me now I know not. I am unpardoned in England, and my poor estate consumed; and whether any other prince or State will give me bread I know not.'

He did not know, either, that Winwood had died six months before. To his wife he wrote on 22nd March, 1618:

' I was loth to write, because I knew not how to comfort you; and God knows I never knew what sorrow meant till now. All that I can say to you is that you must obey the will and providence of God; and remember that the Queen's Majesty bare the loss of Prince Henry with a magnanimous heart . . . Comfort your heart, dearest Bess; I shall sorrow for us both: and I shall sorrow the less because I have not long to sorrow, because I have not long to live. I refer you to Mr. Secretary Winwood's letter,[1] who will give you a copy of it, if you ask for it. Therein you shall know what hath passed—what I have written by that letter—for my brains are broken and 'tis a torment to me to write, especially of misery.'

In a postscript to that letter, Raleigh added:

' I protest before the majesty of God, that as Sir Francis Drake, and Sir John Hawkins died heart-broken, when they failed of their enterprise, I would willingly do the like, did I not contend with sorrow to comfort and relieve you.'

He went on to describe how he had upbraided Keymis for giving up the search for the mine before all hope of finding it was exhausted, and how Keymis had then committed suicide:

' He shut himself up in his cabin, and shot himself with a pocket pistol, which brake one of his ribs; and finding that it had not prevailed, he thrust a long knife under his short ribs up to the handle, and died.'

[1] i.e. the letter which Raleigh had written to Winwood.

There was really no more to be done, but Raleigh's spirit was unconquerable. His men threatened mutiny when he urged them to follow him on a second expedition up the Orinoco; he wished to undertake it in order either to find his mine or to lay his bones by those of his son. So he sailed to Newfoundland, in the desperate hope of finding his lost Virginian colony and returning to Guiana after he had refitted his fleet. But none would follow him and he was deserted by almost all. On 21st June, 1618, he returned alone to Plymouth in his ship, the *Destiny*, to face whatever fate awaited him.

II

The news of the fight at San Thomé was known in Madrid as well as in London during the month of May, 1618. Gondomar burst into the King's closet at Whitehall with the words, ' Pirates! Pirates! ' He was quieted with the assurance that, if the facts were proved after a judicial inquiry, Raleigh would be handed over to Spain for punishment. An order for Raleigh's arrest had been issued before he reached home, but it was not acted upon at once. He was met by his wife at Plymouth, where he toyed for some days with the idea of escaping to France. He could easily have done so then, for official opinion was divided and embarrassed. Raleigh had become the symbol of the traditional anti-Spanish sentiment of the English people, and popular opinion had at long last swung over heavily to his side. Great sympathy was felt with him, and it was widely and openly expressed. The handing over of the fallen hero to the Spaniards, in accordance with the King's pledge to Gondomar, would hardly, in the circumstances, have been politically possible. For those reasons the authorities would at that time have been quite glad to see him escape, but a strange fatalism had gripped Raleigh, so that he ceased for a time to value his safety. He felt that he was too old to start a new life in a strange land, but as his morale started to recover, a measure of optimism returned. He made out a closely argued case for himself, which he put into the hands of his cousin, Lord Carew, a Privy Councillor. In it, he made the point:

' that Guiana be Spanish territory can never be acknowledged, for I myself took possession of it for the Queen of England by virtue of a cession of all the native chiefs of the country.'

He went on to argue with great cogency that the King, by his former actions, had shown that he accepted the validity of that cession.

Raleigh's arrest was effected by another cousin, Sir Lewis Stukeley, Vice-Admiral of Devon, while he was on the road from Plymouth to London, with his wife and a friend. He was taken back to Plymouth and thence, in response to an order from Whitehall, escorted to London, where he arrived on 7th August, 1618. Raleigh's principal concern at that time was to lay his case before the King. He was engaged accordingly in writing an *Apology for the Voyage to Guiana* which he needed time to complete and polish. Shortly before he reached Salisbury Raleigh persuaded a doctor to give him a sufficiently powerful emetic to enable him to feign illness. He also smeared his skin with an irritant in order to convince Stukeley that he was suffering from a contagious fever. The trick succeeded, and there was a long delay at Salisbury. Raleigh publicly feigned madness, ate grass, and refused all other food. But privately his doctor smuggled bread and mutton into his room, where he was able to complete his *Apology* in comparative peace.

In that work Raleigh repeated his claim that the mine he had discovered was not on Spanish territory, but on territory which belonged legally to the English Crown. The question at issue was one of extreme complexity. Clear proof was unobtainable, but three centuries after Raleigh's first expedition to Guiana, a long-standing dispute between the Governments of Great Britain and Venezuela over the boundaries of British Guiana was submitted to the United States Government for friendly arbitration. The British Foreign Secretary, Lord Salisbury, a descendant of Raleigh's former friend, maintained that the territories in dispute were gold-bearing and, in consequence, of great value. The Venezuelan claim was, of course, derived from Spain, but although the award, in 1895 was substantially in favour of Venezuela, it upheld Raleigh's claim that the territory near Mount Iconuri, in which he believed his gold-mine to be situated, as well as the point on the right bank of the Orinoco at which Keymis, after disembarking, had been attacked by the Spaniards, were never in effective Spanish occupation and that they were, legally, at that time in no-man's-land. It would, of course, be unreasonable to expect that the perplexed and angry human beings who clashed at San Thomé, at the farthest known limit of the world, in January, 1618, should have been influenced by the same considerations as those which determined the award issued nearly three centuries later by a group of dispassionate United States arbitrators. But it is worth noting that the fighting was begun not by the British but by the Spaniards, and that the award of 1895 established, by implication, the fact that Raleigh was not at that time committing a trespass.

In London Raleigh had hoped to be allowed to see the King and to place his *Apology* in his hands. He was refused an audience, but he was not immediately committed to the Tower. He was allowed to go to his own house, with Lady Raleigh. He had come to regret bitterly having let slip the chance to escape which had been his while he was still at Plymouth. He entered at once into relations with French friends and agents in London, and was promised a warm welcome at the French Court. All arrangements were made for a ship to carry Raleigh down the Thames and across the Channel, when a servant of Raleigh betrayed the plan to Stukeley. Under orders from Whitehall Stukeley pretended to be overcome with compassion for his prisoner, who was also his kinsman. He offered to flee with him, and Raleigh, with characteristic lack of suspicion, embraced the offer. He was so desperate at that stage that he was incapable of clear thought. The attempt was made on the night of 9th to 10th August, 1618, but Stukeley had laid his plans. At Greenwich another and more powerful boat came alongside, and Raleigh at last understood. Turning to Stukeley, he said with that dignity which never deserted him:

' Sir Lewis, these actions will not turn out to your credit.'

Stukeley's name was execrated during the two years of life which remained to him; he was justly nicknamed ' Judas ', and ostracized, and he died embittered and insane. Raleigh was held at Greenwich for the remainder of that night, and conveyed in the morning to the Tower.

Pity for Raleigh was stirring everywhere throughout the country, but the Court was pledged to his destruction. The only difficulty was to decide the line on which to proceed. Raleigh could be accused as a traitor, who had accepted a Commission, or planned to accept one, in the service of a foreign power; he could be accused of lying in the matter of his gold-mine for the sake of inducing the Crown to grant him a Commission to proceed abroad; or he could be accused of having violated the terms of his Commission by indulging in a piratical act. The ground was carefully explored by the Crown's

legal advisers, who included Sir Francis Bacon and
Sir Edward Coke. It was clear to them that the
evidence would not justify putting Raleigh again
on trial. The prisoner had proved his mettle at
his trial fifteen years before, and a fresh trial, if it
were a fair one, might do great harm to Anglo-
Spanish relations. The lawyers, accordingly, sug-
gested a simple but ugly legal way out of the
dilemma. They advised that as Raleigh was
already a dead man by virtue of his conviction in
1603, the King should merely revoke the limited
reprieve that had been granted in that year.
They advised further that, in order to quieten
public opinion, there should first be a public hearing
before a Commission of Privy Councillors and
Judges. King James objected to that proposal for
a public hearing:

' We think it not fit, because it would make him
too popular, as was found by experiment at the
arraignment at Winchester, where by his wit he
turned the hatred of men into compassion for him.
Also it were too great honour to him . . .'

It was finally decided to stage a private hearing
behind closed doors, so that anything which came
up of an embarrassing nature could be effectually
suppressed.

In the meantime Raleigh had vainly, on 24th
September, 1618, sought to justify himself in a
letter to the King from the Tower:

' May it please Your Most Excellent Majesty,

' If, in my outward journey bound, I had several

of my men murdered at the Islands (the Canaries) and spared to take revenge; if I did discharge some Spanish barks taken without spoil; if I forebare all parts of the Spanish Indies, wherein I might have taken twenty of their towns on the sea-coast, and did only follow the enterprize which I took for Guiana —where, without any decision from me, a Spanish village was burnt, which was newly set up within three miles of the mine—by Your Majesty's favour I find no reason why the Spanish Ambassador should complain of me. If it were not lawful for the Spanish to murder twenty-six Englishmen, tying them back to back, and then to cut their throats, when they had traded a whole month with them, and came to them on land without so much as a sword amongst them all; and if it may not be lawful for Your Majesty's subjects, being forced by them, to repel force by force, we may justly say, " O miserable English." '

On 15th October, 1618, a formal letter from Philip III of Spain reached James, conveying his wish that Raleigh should be executed in England, and not in Spain, as had been promised. And on 22nd October the private hearing took place. Six days later, on 28th October, Raleigh was led before the Bar of the King's Bench to learn his fate. He was addressed by Sir Henry Yelverton, the Chief Justice:

' Sir Walter Raleigh hath been a statesman and a man who in regard to his parts and quality is to be pitied. He hath been a star at which the world hath gazed. But stars may fall, nay, they must fall when they trouble the sphere wherein they abide.'

Raleigh's continued existence had become, in fact, an obstacle in the path of that policy of friendship and alliance with Spain which James I and his advisers were resolved to pursue. The prisoner was asked if he had anything to say why he should not be put to death on his old conviction for treason in 1603. He was told explicitly that he was not being condemned for any offence committed on his recent voyage, and the Chief Justice thought it desirable to disassociate himself explicitly from any suggestion of prejudice:

'Your religion,' he pompously observed, ' hath been much questioned. But I am resolved that you are a good Christian, for your *History of the World*, which is an admirable work, doth testify as much.'

In reply Raleigh pointed out with spirit that having been commissioned by the King for a voyage overseas with powers of life and death over others, he presumed that he had been discharged from his former conviction. He was informed that he was mistaken. He went on to argue that the King himself had formerly been of the opinion that he had received hard measure. Sir Henry Yelverton gently rebuked him, but conceded that it would have been hard measure to call for execution fifteen years after conviction if new offences had not reminded His Majesty ' to revive what the law hath formerly cast upon you '. He was told that he must die the following day, not by hanging, but be decapitation.

All appeals failed, including one from the Queen, sent through Buckingham, the favourite. Raleigh prepared for death, and he acted his part in the proudest Elizabethan manner. In so doing he turned his execution into a triumph. That morning, on the way from his cell to the King's Bench, he had felt so ill that he had somewhat neglected the combing of his hair and beard. His valet had protested, and Raleigh laughingly asked him if he knew of any plaster that would set a man's head on his shoulders again, after it had been struck off by the axe. On the way back he met an old friend who solicitously asked what had happened. Raleigh told him, and laughingly advised him to come early to Palace Yard in the morning so that he might secure a good place:

' For my part,' he added lightly, ' I am sure of one.'

Raleigh spent his last night in the old Gate House, by Palace Yard, Westminster. Friends came to see him to say farewell, and the Dean of Westminster called, to urge him to make his peace with God. Lady Raleigh came also, and whispered, before she broke down, that she had permission from the Council to dispose of his body:

' 'Tis well, dear Bess, that you should have the disposal of that, dead, which living was so often denied you.'

He left a testamentary note which ended:

'. . . If I had not loved and honoured the King

truly, and trusted in his goodness somewhat too much, I had not suffered death.'

He also left, in his bible, a poem which he had composed; it read:

> *Even such is time, which takes in trust*
> *Our youth, our joys, our all we have,*
> *And pays us but with earth and dust;*
> *Who, in the dark and silent grave,*
> *When we have wandered all our ways*
> *Shuts up the story of our days.*
> *But from this earth, this grave, this dust,*
> *My God shall raise me up, I trust.*

Towards dawn, on 29th October, 1618, the Dean returned to administer the Sacrament. He found Raleigh cheerful, uncomplaining, and quietly confident. He dressed carefully, and walked firmly to the scaffold in Palace Yard. There was a great crowd of spectators. In his dying speech he protested his innocence with modesty and dignity, and begged his audience to pray for:

'a man full of vanity who has lived a sinful life in such callings as have been most inducing to it. I have been a sea-faring man, a soldier, and a courtier, and in the temptations of the least of these there is enough to overthrow a good mind and a good man . . .'

He died, he said, in the faith of the Church of England, hoping for salvation through our Saviour, Jesus Christ:

'So I take my leave of you all, making my peace

with God. I have a long journey to take, and must bid the company farewell.'

The scaffold was cleared and Raleigh knelt down. The executioner asked him to lie facing east, and he remarked:

' What matter which way the head lie, so the heart be right.'

He refused to be blindfolded, saying:

' Think you I fear the shadow of the axe, when I fear not the axe itself.'

After praying for a short while he stretched out his hands as a signal that he was ready. The executioner hesitated:

'What does thou fear? Strike, man, strike! '

Two strokes only were required, and a deep groan burst from the bystanders.

POSTSCRIPT

Raleigh and the Seventeenth Century

RALEIGH'S TRUNK was buried in front of the Communion table at St. Margaret's, Westminster. His head was embalmed and preserved by Lady Raleigh until her death in 1647, aged eighty-two. Her son, Carew, then had it buried. Lady Raleigh received kindness and help from many friends, including Lord and Lady Carew. She was not thrown destitute upon the world, and her son, Carew, was ambitious to recover Sherborne. He never succeeded. He went to Wadham College, Oxford, in 1621, and later, from 1635–39, served Charles I as a gentleman of the Privy Chamber. He represented Haslemere in the House of Commons from 1648–53, and was made Governor of Jersey in 1660.

The sacrifice of Raleigh which King James had made to appease the Spaniards was one of a number of causes of the lasting resentment felt by the seafaring and commercial classes against the Stuart dynasty. Peace with Spain may have been financially necessary, but it was unpopular while it lasted because the Spaniards still claimed to exclude British trade from large parts of the world. Among those who witnessed the execution were two West Countrymen—Sir John Eliot and John Pym, who, later, became bitter enemies of the Stuart monarchy. It has been pointed out that Palace Yard, where Raleigh was beheaded, is only distant by about a quarter of a mile from the place in front of Whitehall where Charles I suffered thirty years later: 'The ghost of Raleigh pursued the House of Stuart to the scaffold.'[1] Only a hundred years, part of which included the whole of Raleigh's life, divided the death of Henry VIII in 1547, at the height of his tyranny and pride, from the execution of 'the man, Charles Stuart', in 1649 at the hands of rebel sectarian fanatics.

Raleigh's life affords a late but superb example of a renaissance career passed on the island, off the edge of the Continent, which was the last to be fertilized by the myriad intoxicating influences of the great European renaissance. That life, which enshrined a strange intensity of experience, excluded the qualities of prudence and moderation which could have saved their possessor from ruin. No place existed for Raleigh amid the peaceful and corrupt prosperity of Jacobean England. The era of high adventure was ended, but in the eyes of plain men and women he symbolized the spirit of his race and nation far more truly than any of his

[1] G. M. Trevelyan, *History of England*, 388.

smooth supplanters did at the unpleasant and pedantic Court of James I.   As an extraordinary flower of Elizabethan individualism he earned undying fame.   His faults and his virtues both stemmed from that source.   They were keyed to a pitch of uninhibited magnificence which has rarely been paralleled.   The vivid, gorgeous blossom of Raleigh's hot-house individualism lit up the life of England for many years.   Its intoxicating odour has been wafted down the centuries, but the plant was too exotic to take deep root in the soil.   It became overshadowed by a suffocating growth of religious and secular controversy, as the problems which the Elizabethan Government had evaded or postponed came up for settlement ;   and the Jacobean climate choked and killed.

Chronological Table

Events in Raleigh's Life	General Events
1552 Birth at Hayes Barton, Devon	1553 Death of Edward VI. Accession of Mary I
	1559 Reformation Church settlement
1568 At Oriel College, Oxford	
1569 In France, at battle of Montcontour	
1574 Return from France	1570 The Pope excommunicates Elizabeth
1575 Student at Middle Temple	1577 Drake sails round the world
1579 With Sir Humphrey Gilbert in action off Cape Verde	–80
1580 On active military service in –81 Ireland	
1581 Bearer of despatches to the Queen	
1583 Favourite at Court	
1584 M.P. for Devon. Knighted. Patent to colonize Virginia	
1586 Captain of the Guard	
	1587 Execution of Mary, Queen of Scots. Earl of Essex arrives at Court
1589 In Ireland, under a temporary cloud	1588 Defeat of the Spanish Armada. Death of Robert Dudley, Earl of Leicester.
1590 Return to Court and favour.	
1592 Marriage to Elizabeth Throckmorton. Imprisonment in the Tower. Release from the Tower. Banishment from the Court	
1594 Charge of blasphemy and atheism collapses. Recon-	

157

Events in Raleigh's Life	*General Events*

	naissance expedition to Guiana. Birth of son, Walter		
1595	Raleigh's first expedition to Guiana		
1596	*The Discovery of the Large, Rich, and Beautiful Empire of Guiana* published. At the sack of Cadiz		
1597	In action at the Azores. Restoration to favour and return to Court	1601	Rebellion and execution of Essex
1600	Governor of Jersey		
		1603	Death of Elizabeth I. Accession of James I
1603	Arrest of Raleigh and Cobham. Trial for treason. Sentence of death. Sentence suspended		
1603 –16	Prisoner in the Tower		
		1612	Death of Cecil (Earl of Salisbury). Death of Henry, Prince of Wales
1605	Birth of younger son, Carew		
1614	Publication of *History of the World*	1616	Death of Shakespeare
1616	Release from the Tower		
1617	Second expedition to Guiana		
1618	Fight at San Thomé. Young Walter is killed. Raleigh lands at Plymouth. Arrest and execution	1647	Death of Lady Raleigh